Transfer your
game to the course!

Enjoy,

Jeff Warne

Golf Scrimmages
Realistic Practice Games Under Pressure

Trent Wearner

© copyright 2006 by Trent Wearner

All rights reserved. No part of this publication may be reproduced in any form or by any other means, without written permission of the author. Contact the author at TrentWearnerGolf.com

ISBN-13: 978-0-9787502-0-6
ISBN-10: 0-9787502-0-9

Printed in the United States

It is with much love that I dedicate this book to my wife Robyn, with whom I enjoy spending all the joys of life, as well as our parents, Glenn and Nancy Wearner and Gary and Judy Nye. Thank you for all of your love and support. Thanks also to my Uncle Joel Taylor, PGA Member and former tour professional, for giving me my first bag of clubs.

This book would not have happened if it weren't for my students. It means a great deal to me to witness your enjoyment and progress in the game. Thanks for letting me be a part of your fun.

Table of Contents

Acknowledgments   iii

Introduction   v

Chapter 1	**A Balanced Approach to Improving** *A sound guide to looking at your own game*	Page 1
Chapter 2	**Scrimmages** *A technique used in other sports*	Page 8
Chapter 3	**The Range Is Not The Course** *Turn the practice facility into the golf course*	Page 15
Chapter 4	**Practice Under Pressure** *Turn up the heat*	Page 21
Chapter 5	**Training Mechanics vs. Practicing Golf** *The percentage of practice time between the two*	Page 24
Chapter 6	**Are You Ready?** *What you'll need to play these games*	Page 29
Chapter 7	**Putting Games**	Page 31
Chapter 8	**Chipping Games**	Page 91
Chapter 9	**Pitching Games**	Page 135
Chapter 10	**Bunker Games**	Page 169
Chapter 11	**Full Swing Games**	Page 187
Chapter 12	**On-Course Games**	Page 207
	Trent Wearner Golf *About the Author*	Page 231

Acknowledgments

THE WONDERFUL GAME OF GOLF has taken my wife and me to some unforgettable places and I have been extremely fortunate to have taught side-by-side with some of the best instructors in the nation. Great mentors, co-workers and students have had such a positive impact on my career. All are my friends and I value the experience of working with each one of them.

Thank you to Keith Lyford and Mike McGetrick as well as my fellow teaching professionals Tom Talbott, Tim Odegard, Dana Smith and Steve Heany.

A very special thank you to Jerry Walters and Bob Ottewill for your guidance and friendship.

Thank you Hayes Colburn for your expertise and timeliness.

I would like to thank Titleist and Scott Freelove as well as FootJoy and Tom Krystyn. Your support is greatly appreciated.

A big thank you to Mike Lynch and Tehama. No one does corporate golf better than Corporate Golf Incentives (www.cgigolf.com).

A special thanks to The Golf Club at Bear Dance where the cover photo was taken as well as Meridian Golf Club, Green Gables Country Club and El Conquistador Country Club where the photographs for all of the games were shot.

Introduction

PRACTICE IS A PROCESS USED to develop a skill. It is a tool that should lead toward improvement. In golf, practice should ultimately produce players who are well-rounded and better prepared for any on-course situation and competition. With practice comes the hope that lower scores and a more consistent game are on the horizon. Unfortunately, a multitude of golfers don't experience such benefits.

This is in large part due to the overwhelming tendency to relate practice only to *mechanics* while the development of *playing skills* goes by the wayside. While it is absolutely true that numbers of golfers need to improve their mechanics, it is not the entire picture. A balance between *mechanical improvements*, developing a strong *mental game and on-course skills* as well as making the most of your time through the use of *practice games* is a more meaningful way to look at improving.

> *Most golfers spend their whole lives trying to develop a repeating swing, as if mechanics alone will make them good players. I learned early on there is more to golf than that.*
>
> *--Phil Mickelson*

Hitting ball after ball without a goal, a consequence or a feeling similar to what you'll experience on the course is not sensible. Putting multiple balls without any pressure involved or carelessly chipping or pitching a bunch of balls to a hole isn't preparation for the actual event. Training in the form of repetitions is commonly accepted when developing mechanical improvements but should not dominate your practice especially once those improvements have been acquired. The endless search for some sort of perfect swing, the over consumption of advice and constantly practicing from a level lie is far from what the game is about. Being able to adapt to different lies and various terrain, having a plethora of shots in your bag, getting over mishits or misfortune and experiencing a variety of situations is more realistic and is what you'll encounter from shot to shot, hole to hole, round to round and course to course.

Unrealistic practice breeds **inconsistency** and the **inability to transition good shots in practice to the course**. Even great shots in practice are often a façade and don't necessarily translate into great shots and lower scores while playing. This can be extremely frustrating but blame can't be directed at the golf course itself. It is the unrealistic practice environment and purposeless practice process that needs to be transformed.

The Missing Link

In order to play better golf, you should practice how you play or how you'd *like* to play. As it is in other sports, practice in golf should be in preparation for competition, the field of play and the feel of play. Ironically, the shots and emotions you experience on the course seldom, if ever resemble what occurs in practice and therein lies the problem … or opportunity.

If you want to be more consistent on the course, the shots you hit in practice should be inconsistent. That's right – inconsistent. The types of shots must differ just as they do on the course. If you happen to consecutively hit the same club or shot in practice, while less realistic, pressure applied through the use of consequences, goals or a scoring system can dramatically boost your on-course play. Your practice must simulate the golf course physically, mentally and emotionally. Most players don't have the luxury to learn solely on the course, so what golfers are left with is transforming the practice facility into a more realistic environment. All of this is accomplished by incorporating realistic situations under pressure into your practice through the use of **competitive practice games** or **golf scrimmages**.

This book is a practical source containing nearly one hundred competitive practice games. Many have multiple versions or variations and they fall into six basic categories: putting games, chipping games, pitching games, bunker games, full swing games, and on-course games. You can make many of these games as easy or as difficult as you wish which makes them effective for the novice as well as the professional.

These games demand or require either by their set rules or by you - and this is the most important part - that the lie, your stance and the shot vary and that you alternate the target and change clubs often. Through your own chosen goal or a scoring system, your shots will now emulate playing in situations which evoke pressure and this, along with various circumstances, creates realism. This develops a purpose for and benefit to every shot that is hit whether it is a full swing, short shot or putt and is what will help you get the most out of your practice transforming your game into one that is well-prepared for the course and competition. Depending on your level of dedication, you can even add practice sessions in various weather conditions. But regardless of your ability level or degree of dedication, to get the most out of your practice and learning, it must eventually be done in a realistic outdoor setting.

Benefits

Playing these games promotes several skills. Your ability to recover mentally from missed shots should be acquired and you should attain the physical skills to hit a wide array of shots. At the same time, they will help sharpen your attitude and your desire. You will become a more effective thinker and mentally stronger as you develop strategic thinking, sound risk-reward analysis and mental toughness. In order to improve in these areas though, you need to be aware of your actions, your frame of mind and your approach. Don't let a poor attitude hinder your ability to gain experience during practice.

Through playing golf scrimmages, you'll come to understand how they'll help your competitive on-course spirit. Your overall confidence will rise along with your inner will power to get the ball in the hole - and in a fewer number of strokes than you ever have before – those are playing skills. As Lee Trevino once said, "Just figure out a way to get it in the hole, no matter what it looks like." He also said that he got his confidence from hard work and that hard work was in the form of practicing realistically not without purpose and mindlessly beating balls on the range.

As realistic practice comes to the forefront of your practice regimen, you'll also learn how to effectively use your practice facility. You'll understand how easy it is to simply incorporate the various games in this book into your practice and efficiently match a game or two to what you need to work on within your game. It will become apparent how productive and fun such practice is as you become a more skillful player teaching yourself new shots along the way. Your practice will be more useful and purposeful. You will walk away from each practice session with a sense of accomplishment, knowing you're doing something great for your game. You may even find that you play better than you practice. After all, you practice so that you can sink that final putt to win the club championship or a major championship, beat your friend for the first time or shoot your lowest score ever.

The Target … Audience

People obviously play and compete for different reasons. Many enjoy the sport for the camaraderie and others enjoy it for the personal challenges that it presents. For some it may mean breaking 100 for the first time or just playing without being embarrassed. For others, competition is their weekend league, junior golf association tournament, college golf, the tour qualifying school or major golf championship. Whatever competing means to you, practicing these games will help you take a more accomplished and intuitive game to the golf course.

Whether you're a junior golfer or adult, amateur or professional, the games in this book will hone or develop your on-course skills and turn you into a player of the game. If you're a golf coach or instructor, this book consists of practical tools that provide more meaningful, fresh and efficient guidance for your players or students. Incorporation of these games into your practice or the practice of your students or players will construct a bridge between the practice tee and the first tee. No matter your level of competition they promote challenging situations in practice so the actual game on the course is more familiar to you and perhaps even easier.

What Lies Ahead

The series of chapters which precede the nearly one hundred competitive practice scrimmages begins with an effective way to look at improving your game. It is a balanced approach to bettering the aspects of your game that need attention. Also within these chapters, your understanding of the necessity to practice realistically will be confirmed. You will learn how the range and the course drastically differ but more importantly, you'll learn how to turn the entire practice facility into a practical and beneficial arena as well as the general percentage of time that you should allocate to training your mechanics compared to practicing the game of golf. You will learn how athletes in other sports practice and prepare for a game and how they incorporate scrimmages and other game-like scenarios into their practice regimen. The chapter on pressure should make it apparent that infusing pressure into your practice is an invaluable component to successfully transitioning your game to the course. Overall, these chapters should help better explain how incorporating scrimmages into your practice will help bridge the gap between practice and play.

Chapter 1

A Balanced Approach to Improving

Happiness is not a matter of intensity, but of balance and order and rhythm and harmony.
-- Thomas Merton

It is important to keep all of the things in your life in a personal balance. This balance must be healthy to you and to those around you. The same approach should also be found in your golf game. Clearly, an area of your game which is inflating your scores deserves more attention than others. For instance, it doesn't pay to be a great ball striker if your short game is suspect. The opposite is also true; a great short game, though it can make up for a lot, can't make up for hitting your tee ball out of bounds or deep into the woods on most holes. After recognizing the shots that are a source of trouble, golfers should look to those areas and work to improve them. But don't stop there.

Look further than the common areas of putting, chipping, pitching and full swing mechanics. Look to the quality of your practice. Investigate mental techniques that will enhance your abilities on the course. Sound game management and effective strategies should also be developed. As a teaching professional it is my job to visibly improve the games of my students and to do that, I have to be versed in many areas. I must be able to decipher exactly the difficulties of my students, communicate to them and present a clear improvement process.

This all-encompassing approach to teaching and coaching includes **mechanical improvements**, the development of **on-course skills and mental habits** and the understanding of **proper practice**. Crafting a game improvement plan means having balance in all of these areas.

Mechanical Improvements

The student must have an accurate concept of the improvement he or she is seeking. The concept, mechanical improvement and learning process must be understood by the student. This is of course dependent on the instructor's ability to explain things on a level understandable by the student and in a plethora of ways if need be. It must be made clear to the student and teacher where the plan of instruction will take the student. Without a clear and effective game plan, the likelihood of improving diminishes greatly. The team of student and teacher should write down the mechanical goal followed by the path that you both intend to take in order to get there. Though certain steps of this path may not be set in stone, review of this charted goal and the step by step process to be followed should be reviewed at every lesson.

The teacher must become aware of any physical limitations or flexibility issues the student may have. It does absolutely no good to try to work on something if the student cannot physically move there and it may cause further injury. An alternate route or workout regimen may need to be discussed.

It is also vital that the student's equipment be properly fit. The club can dictate the motion made by the student. Such knowledge by your instructor can greatly speed up the improvement process.

Each aspect of your game should be proficient and your practice should be reflected in that. You should know how to hit all the shots you encounter during a round. If you have trouble with a particular shot, then you should seek out your teaching professional.

> *When you have balance, you're going to be more successful.*
>
> -- *Tiger Woods*
> *Golf Digest, February 2006*

If you are on a structured path of improving your mechanics with a teaching professional, continue on that process. Those who spend the time and money to effectively improve their mechanics by seeking out quality professional instruction are to be applauded. When you do work on your mechanics, know that feel and awareness are vital. Repetitions are also crucial but not if they're performed lazily. Once you lose your focus, it's time for something else. Take a break, practice another part of the game or simply go home. You need to be aware of when your focus becomes ineffective.

> *All my life I've tried to hit practice shots with great care. I try to have a clear-cut purpose in mind on every swing. I always practice as I intend to play. And I learned long ago that there is a limit to the number of shots you can hit effectively before losing your concentration on your basic objectives.*
>
> *-- Jack Nicklaus*

ON-COURSE SKILLS & MENTAL HABITS

These are non-mechanical and yet unusually simple ways to better your game. While time and awareness are needed for new habits to be formed, these techniques will make your scores lower and more consistent. Matter of a fact, in addition to mechanical improvements, these are some of the most "ah ha" or enlightening moments our students have. They can't believe they've played the game for so long and never thought of or applied these processes into their game.

Some of these skills and habits revolve around game and self management. One example is having the discipline to watch your ball until it stops. This should be done with regard to a full shot, a short game shot and a putt both in practice and in play. Around the green, get used to watching each chip shot until the ball stops. Witnessing the break that the ball takes will raise the chances of making the putt you're now faced with. On the course, it's inevitable during a playing lesson to witness a student hit his ball into the native grass and not watch it land.

Instead, the student turns around disgusted with the shot he just hit. As we approach the area where he thinks he hit his ball, I let him lead the way. After I see he's not even close, I walk the student sometimes fifty yards to the actual location of his ball. Students are often amazed how quickly I can find their golf ball. But it's so simple – you just have to watch it and pick a reference point in which to direct your search. This lack of discipline is the reason why it takes groups forever to look for golf balls. Valuable time has been wasted, aggravation is elevated, a ball is lost and a stroke and distance penalty will likely be incurred. Unless you are on tour where a wall of people often keep your ball from going too far out of play, own up to your shots by precisely watching where they come to rest. Don't depend on your partners or friends to watch. Bad shots are a part of the game and no big deal. Your reactions to them though are.

Other on-course skills include becoming your own coach. This means knowing what to do if your game goes south. Depending on the severity, it may mean playing the remainder of your round with a particular miss or knowing what to do to reduce or eliminate it. You also need to know how to strategize and properly calculate risk-reward situations. You must fuel yourself appropriately, be strong mentally and have a routine that suits you and allows you to perform at your highest.

These are just a few examples. There are many topics within on-course instruction. What is delivered to the student completely depends on the issues of each student. While some of these can be taught on the practice area, if you've never taken a playing lesson before, you should discuss taking one with your teaching professional. Strategies, new perspectives and effective thinking can make a dramatic improvement in your score.

I believe so highly in this that I often take the time to watch my students, especially juniors, play in local tournaments in order to get a better understanding of their habits. With that understanding, I can help further the awareness and discipline of their routines, make their practice rounds more effective and help them productively manage themselves and their game.

Proper Practice

Practicing wisely mainly consists of two categories and the percentage of time that you should spend on each. These two categories are *training one's mechanics* and *practicing golf*. First identifying target areas, then mechanically understanding the improvements and how to work on them so that you can be certain your training time is useful.

The second part is the content within this book. You need to learn to practice in an environment that resembles playing. It's about having sound practice sessions that translate to the golf course. One of my favorite golf quotes is, "After we learn to swing like Hogan, we still have to learn how to play like him." While the author of this quote is unknown, it has enormous weight to it. In place of Hogan's name, fill in your favorite player, or any player and the meaning still has tremendous merit.

Also within *Proper Practice* comes the understanding of how to prepare for a tournament and what to accomplish during a practice round. A routine found in preparing for a tournament and the process of a practice round is individually based. Everyone has a different personality and approach to learning and playing their best. No one really prepares exactly the same. Your pre-tournament routine and on-course game should be unique to you.

This general philosophy of mechanical improvements, developing on-course skills and mental habits and learning a proper practice method may be seen as a blanket approach but the tools and information that fall within each category are approached individually. Nothing is automatically applied to every student that comes to the golf academy. As a matter of a fact, most of my students have no idea of such a philosophy. We work on what is relevant to each one of their games. Each person is at a different place in his or her game and the information presented reflects that. The instruction, communication and coaching differ with each person. My current students are offered a game tracking spreadsheet to use if they'd like, which can help us monitor each aspect of their game. With new students, I never know what I'm going to be doing until we, student and teacher, find out more about the student's game, learning style, goals and the like. The individuality of it all is the joy and essence of teaching.

The only one-for-all-approach that I use in my teaching is the use of a questionnaire. Everyone must complete one. To teach someone, with any level of relevance, to improve their setup or swing without knowing some pertinent information about them is nearly impossible. In order to connect with the student, the instructor needs to know the student's current setup, swing and concepts, allotted practice time, goals, purpose for playing and any physical limitations the student may have. Understanding any concerns they may have demonstrates care and compassion and it calms any anxieties they may bring to the lesson.

From their answers, comes vital information that will help me immensely. After that, the instruction and coaching will be unique to that person. In order for the highest level of learning to occur, the information presented should empower the student and be individually suited to each person.

> *The only way in which one human being can properly attempt to influence another is by encouraging him to think for himself, instead of endeavoring to instill ready-made opinions into his head.*
>
> *--Leslie Stephen*

I believe that teaching is both an art and science. Though there is definitely science involved in the learning styles of people, knowing what to say, how to say it and when to say it is the art of connecting with another human being. Each person learns differently to some degree and it is the job of the teaching professional to clearly and concisely convey the appropriate message. I have to be very basic and picture-oriented with some students while others require me to be extremely technical and mechanical with them. Time together with my students will definitely be fun but along the way I may need to be direct at times. I must challenge them, inspire them, encourage them, coach them, support them and certainly empower them. It is my goal that each student play at a level he or she wishes to under pressure, on the course, on their own and consistently.

Golf instruction is a delicate process that requires two-way communication between the team of instructor and student. There is no easy rule for finding the right instructor for you. You must do some research, ask around and interview several instructors before you make an investment and a decision to entrust your game with a particular professional. If you are looking for a teaching professional to assist and guide you, you should sit down with this person and ask questions as you would your doctor. An interview will likely confirm if the teacher's style is flexible enough to match yours. Find someone who is truly interested in you and your game and who has the experience, ability and training to translate that interest into measurable improvement.

chapter 2

SCRIMMAGES

*We improve ourselves by victories over oneself.
There must be a contest, and we must win.*

-- Edward Gibbon

SCRIMMAGING IS AN INFORMAL practice technique used to simulate a real game and whatever the sport, they help players and coaches gain an understanding of how the game atmosphere affects the players. They provide a clearer picture of the adaptability of each player, the team as a whole and the plays and shots they choose to perform. Scrimmaging allows the athlete to drop any mechanically induced movements and put trust in his or her training so that the motion becomes more effective and less thought provoked or thoughtless altogether. While scrimmages are commonplace in other sports, they are missing in the practice sessions of most golfers. The games in this book however allow you to fill that void. These games are in golf, like scrimmages are in team sports.

MENTAL AND EMOTIONAL ASPECTS

Scrimmaging sets the stage for the game. It involves distractions similar to what will be experienced come game time. Think about all of the distractions around you when you hit balls or practice your short game at your practice facility. Other people swing or putt at the same time and very close to you. People walk behind you and to each side. Balls are poured on the ground and range baskets clank against each other. A group is repeatedly called to the first tee over the intercom and people are constantly talking to one another or on a mobile phone.

These distractions are beautiful challenges which seldom bother you as you hit ball after ball on the range. You accept and expect them. As soon as you set foot on the course though, the slightest noise or movement can set you off. If this is true for you, you need to expect and accept disruptions on the course as well or better yet, be so entranced in what you're doing that they seem to have disappeared. If your practice begins to represent the mentality of being on the course, this ability to accept and zone out distractions will carry over. Use the distractions of the range to test your on-course skills and the strength of your routine. If you can get into a game-like mode with all of that going on, playing on the course will seem elementary. Things won't bother you as much or at all.

Jerry Rice, the greatest receiver in NFL history, once noted that he didn't hear any crowd noise at all when he caught or ran with the football. Throughout his career, he worked on aspects of the game which would help him catch, run and block better in a game. He worked on things he had control over. By preparing himself better than other players, he became the best at his craft.

Next time you're at a practice facility, evaluate what you do on the driving range and putting green and watch other golfers practice. You'll come to understand that the emotions felt there do not simulate what you feel on the course, that what is typically done in practice isn't the most effective process for a successful transition to the course. You'll realize that the missing link to *playing* better is a proper balance between improving mechanically and practicing realistic situations under pressure. Like athletes in other sports, you need to plan for the game and practice for the game. You need to scrimmage.

> *More men fail through lack of purpose than lack of talent.*
>
> -- Billy Sunday

Other Sports' Take On Practice

Teams in the NFL spend an enormous amount of time and money simulating game situations in practice. Take for example, the Denver

Broncos, whose home field is an outdoor stadium with natural grass. If their upcoming game is on artificial turf at an indoor stadium, the Broncos utilize that part of their practice facility consisting of an indoor field with artificial turf. The Broncos alter their environment and equipment to match the playing conditions; they even pipe in crowd noise to simulate the noise level of their rival's fans. They've constructed such a facility so they can practice in the conditions in which they're going to play. All of those practice characteristics assist with the sensation of actually being there in the game. It takes the "surprise" out of game day so as to raise the performance level of each player and team.

Tom Brady, quarterback for the New England Patriots was the seventh string quarterback at Michigan. The scouting consensus was that he was skinny, slow and had a weak arm. But at the age of twenty-four he became the youngest quarterback at that time to win a Super Bowl and at the age of twenty-eight had three Super Bowl rings. Prefacing his interview with Brady on *60 Minutes*, Steve Croft said, "He (Brady) spends hours in the tape room looking at opposing teams so that he can visualize what's going to happen and where people are going to be before the ball is ever snapped." Brady went on to say, "A lot of it's spending the time in here on the film trying to get as many pictures in your head before the game as you can so when you do walk on the field you can just verify what's going on. It's not like you just go out there and wing it."

While golf isn't football, the point is that Brady's preparation for his team's opponent is thorough – that he practices for the game and such devotion is reflected in his success. Relating it to golf, you can substitute an opposing football team for the golf course you're about to play. When at a practice facility you can play the golf course on the range or you can even play the golf course mentally if you're not at a practice facility.

Basketball players run plays and scrimmage during most of their practice. They create situations that set them up for what an opposing team may throw at them. Since the basket and playing court do not change, players have to prepare themselves for the opposition and their tendencies. They don't practice set shots from the field, let alone repetitively, because that shot is unrealistic. But that "set shot" is done on driving ranges everywhere day after day.

While baseball players have a hitting coach, the majority of their time is spent in the batting cage where they are thrown a variety of pitches. Major league hitters don't conduct batting practice with a tee. A viable technique must be adaptable to different pitches from different pitchers. The batter has to learn to read the pitch in order to consistently hit the ball. If hitters practiced by swinging the bat over the plate at only one height, which is much like what golfers do on the range, they wouldn't be very effective. The batter too has to adapt and be versatile but that's what really makes hitting a baseball or golf ball so much fun.

Proper Practice

These games will fittingly prepare you for the numerous physical and mental situations that can be found when playing. Tiger Woods wrote in his book, *How I Play Golf*, "It (the psychology of golf) entails mental toughness, self-confidence, intimidation, gamesmanship, conquering inner demons, instant recall of past successes and being able to quickly purge failures. It is the game within the game." While some golfers seem to have been born with such attributes, most need to work on them and will see progress in their game if they do. Applying appropriate mental techniques into your game is an important process and an eye-opening experience. Such techniques can be made light of during a playing lesson and through practice that resembles playing.

Realistic practice isn't accomplished by hitting multiple balls to the same target or hole without any pressure involved or a goal established. While it may prove that you can hit the shot, this type of practice is not in preparation for the actual event and one major key to gaining confidence is your level of preparation for what you will experience on the course. Giving yourself a mulligan is a false sense of confidence and it certainly doesn't allow you to embrace a pressure situation. Take the "do overs" out of your practice and out of your game. The common act of rolling three balls on the practice putting green doesn't help when it comes time to do it once on the course and it doesn't promote reading the putt. Perhaps unknowingly, you may use the first or second putt as your gauge as you roll a great third putt and then wonder why reading a putt on the course is such a mystery.

Scrimmaging and the actual event don't demand perfection. They demand versatility which is why you shouldn't always prop the ball on a perfect lie time and time again when practicing. While such an activity may be acceptable when working on your mechanics, a more realistic route will eventually be needed to test your technique. Instead, you should drop it or roll it over from the pile and hit it from where it lies. This will help you to learn how to physically hit the shot and mentally be prepared for it when it occurs on the course. When a professional golfer walks up to his or her ball on the golf course and finds it to be sitting deep down in the rough or in a divot, his or her expression doesn't change. The accomplished player has seen and practiced this lie under pressure countless times. The professional begins to strategize a plan for what can be done with this shot and picks an appropriate target. For the everyday golfer faced with the same situation, it is a lack of realistic practice that sets off negative emotions and therefore the tendency to conjure up another bad shot often times blaming it on the condition of the course or constant bad luck.

In other sports, participants are physically, mentally and emotionally ready because they practice on the same surface in which they play. Therefore they're more familiar with the various situations of the game. In practicing golf, you tend to take yourself out of the real situation more than you put yourself in it. Many people don't have the opportunity to practice on the course but they still practice, so much so that stand alone driving ranges and very unrealistic indoor centers have become ubiquitous in many cities across the country. While there can be great benefits to training your swing indoors or even without a ball, eventually you've got to put it to use in a realistic setting. PGA Tour player and Ryder Cup player Jeff Maggert would certainly agree. He says he doesn't spend much time on the range at all. Instead he practices a lot on the course.

In other sports athletes spend more time simulating the game situation by scrimmaging or running plays than they do trying to get "perfect form." In golf we'd be better off doing the same thing, spending more time imitating course conditions and being creative. Ironically, as golfers progress, they realize that their setup and swing should change for the situation at hand. Accomplished players become accomplished because they alter their setup and swing for the shot at hand. This is also true for the short game. There are many setup and swing factors that can be considered when needing to hit shots with varying spin, trajectory, roll, curve and the like. Tiger Woods, for instance, uses four different grips when hitting shots around the green.

What's At The Root?

While golf tournament television commentators do talk about aspects of a tour pro's game outside of his or her swing mechanics, swing mechanics are often the only thing heard by viewers throughout the telecast. And it sure seems that swing mechanics dominate the time between the telling of how the tournament is played out. There are slow motion scenes and drawings that would impress John Madden. Often times though, the root cause of a particular swing issue comes down to a lack of commitment, a poor plan, bad club selection, a mental mistake or a combination of these. In other words, while all golfers have habits and tendencies, a physical misfire can commonly be traced back to something else. The opposite also holds true then. Mistakes of course will happen but it is a tour pro's mental strength, emotional stability and competitive experience that direct their body physically into performing so well.

Without question there are many tour pros who work on their swing mechanics but they do it at the right time. A change, or improvement as I like to call it, is based on their tournament schedule and the severity of the problem. Tiger Woods' personal quest and need for stimulation drives him to constant improvement of his *entire* game and while much has been made of his swing mechanics it is his mental strength and body awareness that have made him an unbelievable player.

> *I believe that my creative mind is my greatest weapon.*
>
> *-- Tiger Woods*
> *How I Play Golf, 2001*

Annika Sorenstam has admitted the same of her game and it is not a coincidence that creativity and realistic practice consume much of the practice time of the top players in the world. But, I would be misleading you if I told you this is the golden ticket - that competitive practice games are the answer for everything. Even the most intelligently planned practice sessions likely won't prepare you for all that a round of golf will throw at you. However you may be prepared enough to do damage control avoiding big numbers along the way that scar your scorecard. Such control helps your scores stay more consistent from day to day. The unrealistic setting and feelings of whacking ball after ball at a practice facility, without consequences, just won't cut it and having great mechanics or technique alone won't guarantee lower scores.

An athlete could work to hone their technique until the end of time, and still miss the mark.
  --Dr. Fran Pirozzolo

Chapter 3

THE RANGE ≠ THE COURSE

It is not the same to talk of the bulls as to be in the bullring.

-- Spanish Proverb

THE GAME YESTERDAY AND TODAY

TREMENDOUS ADVANCEMENTS HAVE been made in the game of golf. Equipment technology, instruction, video analysis, fitness, and the condition of courses are some. But something noticeable about the game of golf that hasn't really changed for the better is the lack of resemblance practice facilities have with golf courses.

Many early courses actually never had a driving range. The lack of a practice facility meant that golfers had to learn on the course. Consequently they gained invaluable experience. They learned to adapt and they learned what it took to get it in the hole – talents so necessary yet typically overshadowed these days by homogenized instruction, the lifelong pursuit of a machine-like golf swing and unrealistic practice. While a minimal number of people still practice on the course, this once common tradition is quite rare today and it is probably the reason why golfers don't consider course management and playing lessons until much later in their learning process.

If you do have the luxury of being able to get on the course to practice by all means do. This can often happen very early in the morning or late in the evening. In the *On-Course Games* chapter of this book, there are several challenging games to play on the course that will aid in your ability under the gun.

It's unquestionable that the game has made some extraordinary advances that have helped golfers. But the fact of the matter is, the majority is wondering why all these advances and practice hasn't resulted in lower scores. Coming to the realization that there is more to the game than hitting perfect shots will benefit you greatly. Matter of a fact, it's about the poor shots that you hit and how you react and recover when the ball doesn't go where you had intended. Trouble lurks around every corner of a golf course regardless of your ability. The accomplished player knows how to recover and therefore saves several strokes during a round. It's about managing yourself and your shots and giving one hundred percent commitment to each shot you hit. Because the game embodies physical, mental and emotional components of you, your practice should be an integration of them. Practicing realistically under pressure – the golf scrimmages in this book – is that integration.

A New Look On An Old Habit

I encourage you to change what you call "the range." Instead of *range* or *driving range* you can call it a *practice course, practice facility,* or *golf facility*. I once heard golf commentator Ian Baker-Finch call it a *practice fairway* during the telecast of the 2003 Nissan Open at Riviera while Mike Weir was staying loose after his final round awaiting a playoff, which he eventually won, against Charles Howell III.

Renaming "the range" should encourage you to practice how you play. From a book written by Michael Hebron, *Golf Swing Secrets … And Lies*, "Studies show imagination and intuition are probably the best tools for learning a sports skill, with memorization the lowest form." On top of what these games create, you should begin to think about ways you can "play golf" in your practice sessions. You can do this with a visual picture in your mind of what a golf hole looks like. You can create boundaries, hazards, trees and the like with the objects that are on the practice facility or in the background. You can also do this by hitting shots on the practice facility as well as on and around the putting green as you would on the course by going through your physical and mental routine, putting pressure on yourself with a scoring system, placing the ball in an awkward lie and by not hitting the same club twice in a row.

> *We can begin to experience fulfillment as soon as we choose to create an environment permitting us to do so.*
>
> --Bob Samples

A key component to playing great golf is your ability to adapt or adjust to new situations and the ever changing environment. Much of your success is dependent on your preparation and how well you handle problems as they arise. The golf course is an obstacle course that has consequences typically in the form of additional strokes. The typical "range" has neither formidable obstacles nor consequences though the games in this book help create them. Tall pines lining the fairway, thick grass or desert that encroach upon many of your tee shots, bunkers and water hazards strategically positioned by a trained architect are not part of the picture at most practice facilities. The "range" is also wider than the typical fairway and there are piles of chances sitting there on the ground. The level surface of the practice tee, your feet evenly placed and the ball perched up perfectly time after time create a disconnect from the course as such an environment has very little similarity to the shots you must perform when playing. Because of this, your practice could be taking you a step backward. This may be evident in your score, your inability to adapt or recover, your inhibitions or the excuses you make that this unrealistic environment affects your play on the course.

The game of golf is played outdoors and because of this you will encounter an infinite number of situations. Your practice should also be done outdoors. Practice that simulates playing will help develop the skills needed to deal with the multitude of predicaments that the game throws your way.

The golf course is about playing – figuring out a way to get your ball and yourself around the course. You should enjoy that trek as each day presents a new challenge. Most golfers find it easy to get tense, flustered and unorganized on the course. Understandably so when your preparation revolves around a practice arena that doesn't look, sound or feel anything like the course you play. The best situation for golf course architects occurs when they receive the authority to design the golf course and practice facility before the housing and community plotting happens. Unfortunately, it's common for the opposite to occur. Consequently, at times, the golf course and practice facility layout take a backseat and suffer. However, what golfers are left with can still be utilized effectively. At the same time, it's easy to get drawn back into the mindless practice mold so many golfers fall into. Hitting ball after ball without a goal or consequence is commonplace and the blame resides on the shoulders of the person practicing. Such practice misdirects you from the course environment and certainly tournament golf.

A Practical Practice Approach

Practicing on the course may not be suitable for your time schedule, financially possible or accepted by the golf staff due to the number of people playing. This is alright – you just have to use your practice facility wisely just as the world's top golfers do. World-class golfers have learned how to effectively use the practice facility, short game area and putting green. They have eliminated the discrepancy between the "range" and the course through the use of golf scrimmages and with the list of circumstances described below. These circumstances make the practice facility and short game area more meaningful.

Circumstances to be practiced at your facility include:

> *The Lie of the Ball*
>> Practice from the rough, in a divot, tight grass, hard pan, wet grass, from multiple bunker lies and anything you can imagine. Putt from the fringe and when the ball is up against the collar. Try a variety of clubs to see which ones work best for you.
>
> *The Unevenness of the Ground*
>> You should take swings of varying length hitting balls from uphill and downhill lies. Also from lies in which the ball rests above your feet and below your feet. Take note of the ball's flight as each slope will likely create

some sort of different curve or trajectory. Hit shots with one foot in a depression, one foot in the bunker and any combination. You also need to practice putts of varying speed, slope, break and grain.

Elevation

It is necessary to realize, through your experiences during play and practice, how much club to add on or subtract from when the target is above you and when it is below you.

The Elements

Do you know what shots to hit when the wind is present? You need to practice those shots as well as learn how to play, through practicing, in the rain, the cold, and what it's like to play in a rain suit. Can you manage yourself and stay hydrated when it's hot?

Specialty Shots

Often times you'll find yourself needing to hit the ball high, low, or curve it. You'll need to know how to land it soft or have it roll out. During your golf adventures, you'll come across shots where your backswing is abbreviated due to some sort of obstacle.

Emotions

Golfers are constantly feeling pressure, discomfort and uneasiness so you must develop pressure situations in practice in order to become comfortable, confident, practiced, aware, focused, determined and relaxed or perhaps more intense during play on the course.

Routine

Going through the physical and mental steps of your routine in practice is an easy way to get the feel that you're really playing. You should experiment with your routine(s) in order to find out what is the most beneficial process for you. Your practice should include fine tuning your routine and sometimes a change to your routine can make a drastic improvement in your results.

Yardages

It is mandatory that you know the yardage or range

that each of your clubs produce without any outside forces being applied. You should also become aware of how any elements affect those distances as well as learn to hit shots when the yardage falls in-between clubs.

To experience many of a course's physical conditions, you can go to a side of the practice tee where you can hit from contoured terrain or different length grass. Maybe a tree is near the side of the practice tee where you can practice an abbreviated swing missing the trunk or, in order to miss a limb of the tree, a swing of a different shape. If none of this is available, ask your superintendent, general manager or teaching professional to get the ball rolling on developing a place to practice such real situations. It really only takes a mound or two for uneven lies, a small amount of effort to maintain the different lengths of grass for working on shots from the rough and perhaps even a fairway bunker. Of course this takes up space but it is how facilities should be designed and it is sure to bring in more practice facility revenue or impress prospective members.

Through your own personal experiences, I am sure you can add to the list of circumstances described above. The ball and you can be found in an endless number of predicaments certainly more precarious than what golfers do in a typical practice session. Break out of the mindless redundancy brought on by the common practice arena. Practice wisely, realistically and in preparation for as many of these situations as possible.

chapter 4

PRACTICE UNDER PRESSURE

You try to get the pressure on you, you want the pressure on you. You play with it, you enjoy it, because it means you're in contention, have a chance to win.

-- Jack Nicklaus
Majors of Golf, 2001

To get on the course and experience the serenity and beauty so many courses have to offer is a luxury to be savored. Unfortunately, many don't enjoy the experience because their game and scores don't relate to the time that's been devoted to practice. Spending countless hours hitting bottomless buckets of balls does not guarantee lower scores. It should go without saying that what you do on the practice tee, short game area and putting green - the way you practice - has a direct effect on your long-term success, or life-long frustration, in playing the game of golf.

You may know the saying, *If you can't stand the heat, get out of the kitchen.* Well, if you want to get better, you need to get back into the kitchen. As Nicklaus said, you need the pressure. Without pressure being a significant and integral part of your practice time, you're inhibiting your abilities on the golf course. You and your swing do not hold up under pressure on the course because your practice is inconsequential – there's no pressure involved. You develop pressure in practice by setting a goal and having some sort of a scoring system. Both apply pressure to you. These practice games set the stage for such an environment.

Realistic practice under pressure is about creating conditions in practice that allow you to execute the one shot that is in front of you. Its realization will create play on the course that exceeds past performances. Dana Quigley, Champions Tour player, said in the February 2004 issue of *Golf Digest*, "On the course you only get to hit the shot once. That's the key. On the range there is no consequence to a bad shot. You just rake another ball into place and try again."

In the June 2004 issue of *Golf Magazine*, Jim Furyk admitted that his three keys are to "(1) stay sharp after good shots, (2) practice must-make putts and (3) simulate on-course pressure." This is a big reason why, even with his unorthodox swing, Furyk ranked second on Tour in greens in regulation and third in driving accuracy in 2002. He also has an extraordinary record in Ryder Cup play which is said to have the most pressure of any event.

You must apply pressure to your practice sessions and get as used to that pressure as possible. You cannot fight pressure. Furyk invites it and becomes accustomed to it by practicing must-make putts. I would be misleading you if I didn't add the importance of your routine and how it also aids in your ability to get accustomed to the pressure. It is an invaluable tool that should not be overlooked. You need to develop one yourself. A pre-shot routine which helps you properly evaluate the shot and then choose and commit to a target, shot and club. It should be comfortable to you and it must channel your focus to the task at hand. Find and recall mental cues that help you do that. Turn those cues into your trigger so that you know you're in a beneficial frame of mind before you execute each shot.

Denver Bronco Jason Elam, one of the most consistent field goal kickers in the NFL, said on a sports show that he believes in practicing in game-like conditions under pressure. He continued by saying that Coach Mike Shanahan often stands behind him and disturbs him while he's kicking. In practice, he stands back, goes through his routine and pretends he's in a real game. He needs that pressure in practice so that when the game is on the line, distractions become commonplace and his preparation will translate into performance.

The amount of pressure and stress you feel depends on the event and what you tell yourself. You have to spin it positively. Listen to the positive talk of golfers and athletes of other sports. They know that it's all about performing under pressure. It's what they live for.

Tiger Woods certainly understands, along with Elam, that the mental, emotional, and physical aspects of playing need to be attached to practice as well. His creativity and ability to thrive under pressure are in direct relation to his realistic practice process both as a youth and a professional.

> *As a junior golfer I always practiced with my pop. We always played games on the range that were creative and competitive. We did all sorts of things to learn different shots.*
>
> *-- Tiger Woods*

The key word in Tiger's quote is *always*. Some part of his practice always consisted of realistic practice. Although he continues to better his body, his mind and his technique, he purposely experiments. He recently admitted that going into the 2006 season, he has more shots than he used to – to this day he is still learning new shots. And you can bet he's practicing those new shots under pressure.

Junior golfers especially tend to be inventive and creative with their practice. They are superb at this type of pressure-packed practice and it shows in their play, score, quickness in learning and application of improvements. It is not a coincidence that the great players in the world of golf spend a majority of their practice time playing games just like the ones in this book. Greatness seems to come out of people during a competitive practice. It is that component that helps them repeatedly hit that pressure drive or drop that winning putt.

Training Mechanics vs. Practicing Golf

The mechanical movements in golf are not the whole secret.

--Percy Boomer

AN IMPORTANT COMPONENT of practicing properly is the allotted time that is dedicated to **training the mechanics** of your full swing, chipping motion, putting stroke, etc. compared to **practicing the game of golf** or **realistic practice**.

There is a time to train or acquire your mechanics and a time to practice or apply them with little or no thought of them. Your ability to understand the difference between *training* and *practicing golf* can help your practice become more organized and worthwhile. Having the discipline to transition between them at the appropriate times can help a person acquire a swing change more quickly while still being able to effectively play the game.

Many, many golfers have worsened their ability to play the game due to too much mechanical practice. Such practice causes the mind to be dominated by mechanical suggestions on the course. This inhibits your ability to play freely and put your mind where it should be – on the particulars of the shot. Over dominance of swing mechanics is one of the worst sins of trying to improve. In doing so, you can lose your natural talent. You can struggle for quite a while before you realize that such thoughts have erased your desire to get the ball in the hole. I want to stress that there is absolutely nothing wrong with desiring to improve your mechanics. The majority of golfers need quality direction but it is a delicate process that should not be taken lightly by anyone who teaches.

Many golfers' woes can be attributed to inaccurate concepts, poor fundamentals and faulty swing mechanics. Working with golfers on their golf game as a whole with a balanced approach, including improving their mechanics, is what I help golfers do on a daily basis. You simply have to know when it's time to call it quits with your mechanics and transition to a playing mentality. This is where you and an experienced teaching professional develop a plan by discussing your playing schedule, practice time and goals in addition to learning how to practice properly and taking playing lessons.

What Should I Practice?

In general, because you will eventually set foot on the course, it makes sense to spend more of your practice time practicing golf by experiencing realistic situations under pressure. This means 51% or more though 60% is a more commonly recommended minimum percentage.

If you're not mechanically attempting to improve your game, you should spend 80% to 100% of your time practicing realistically. Any time that is not dedicated to mechanics, should be spent constructively experimenting with hitting different shots. Self-discovery is the most empowering of tools we have as curious beings. Try to hit shots that will help you play better, that you can add to your repertoire. If you struggle learning new shots, ask your teaching professional for some advice.

On the other hand, if you're a beginner who struggles to get the ball airborne or a golfer who is taking a large number of penalties due to errant shots, some practice weighted toward improving your mechanics may be necessary but should certainly not be your template for future practice once your ball striking and flight improves.

Ideally you and your teaching professional or coach should develop a personal plan as to this split and the timeframe for which it should continue. Some factors that should be considered include the following:

- *Your short-term goals*
- *Your long-term goals*
- *The type and level of wayward shots you are currently incurring*
- *Any upcoming tournaments*
- *An honest evaluation of your mechanics and if they are truly inhibiting your play*
- *Your off-season commitment*

Some golfers have the ability to work on the mechanical aspects of their game in the days leading up to an event and yet still turn it off by shifting into a playing mentality. They have trust in whatever they bring to the course and they believe that other parts of their game will make up for any part that is lacking. They don't fret; they just play with what they brought. The ability to transition from mechanics to playing is a trait typically found in experienced players but it is something that many over technical golfers could benefit from and should strive to develop.

There are only a few cases when you should be training your swing more than simulating on-course situations and there are simple ways to improve your mechanics without the need to hit zillions of golf balls. The off-season is the best time to make a mechanical improvement. Then you can come out, typically in the spring for most golfers in the country, with better mechanics to apply and begin to trust your new found swing.

Many of my most successful students rarely work on major swing mechanical improvements during the season. Instead we improve playing skills and on-course habits. We develop and hone a sound routine, work on the short game, putt a lot and learn practice methods that encourage better play. The reality however is that most golfers will continuously work toward a mechanically sound swing. During the season is the only time some can commit to such improvements.

But with desire and an understanding of the process it will take based on your issues you can improve significantly. There is nothing wrong with striving to improve and enjoying learning. Your love of learning doesn't always have to revolve around swing mechanics though. There are many other aspects of the game that you can look toward for improvement. You simply need to know when it's time to call it quits with your mechanics and practice as you'd play. You should be able to trust whatever swing you have and take it to the course. But to trust it on the course means you have to spend time trusting it in practice.

Learn From Experience

Don't let the course just be the place where you play. It should also be your stage for learning, where you encompass the atmosphere and embrace the situations and feelings that come with the field of play. To aid in that learning process after each round or tournament, you may find it helpful to write down your answers to the questions below.

Play
1. What did I do well today?
2. What did I learn today?
3. What will I do next time I'm in a similar situation?
4. What do I need to work on before my next round/tournament?

There are also things you should consider writing down in relation to each practice session.

Practice
1. What within my game improvement plan will I accomplish today?
2. What action(s) will I take to make those improvements?
3. How much time will I allocate to these planned items?
4. Did I accomplish my practice plan today?
5. What are my initial thoughts for what I will practice next time?

The important component to answering these questions is that they can be broken down further into three additional categories. You can pose each question three times – one time physically, another mentally and the last emotionally. Answer them in a manner that works for you.

If you're an optimist then keep things positive. If you get energized or motivated by being brutally demeaning to yourself then so be it but in either case and in all the cases in between, be honest with yourself.

Most of my students have a Game Improvement Guide that they use for this as well as tracking their play and practice. It helps organize their game and directs their attention to what needs it most. For more information about a Game Improvement Guide log on to www.TrentWearnerGolf.com.

chapter 6

ARE YOU READY?

To every person there comes in their lifetime that special moment when you are figuratively tapped on the shoulder and offered the chance to do a very special thing, unique to you and your talents. What a tragedy if that moment finds you unprepared or unqualified for work which could have been your finest hour.

--Sir Winston Churchill

THE CHAPTERS THAT FOLLOW are filled with games that should be uncompromising components within your practice sessions. With most of these games, you can compete against your own score. Some require a friend or two but most can be applied alone. Additionally, combining games can be very useful and I encourage you to do so as well as creating your own versions. Most of the games just require that you not forget your clubs but a few of the games can be best utilized if you throw the following easy-to-carry items into your golf bag: scorecards or disks, pennies, Sharpie®, string or the Lag Golf System rings, tailor's measuring tape, tees, a chalk line, a journal, pencil and a shag bag of practice balls if you have one.

The remainder of the book is divided into six chapters and structured so that you can go directly to the chapter that relates to what you need to work on. Use the Table of Contents in the front of the book to find what pages you should turn to in order to match the area of the game with what you need to improve.

The inner workings of each game can continue to challenge you throughout your entire golf career. Each game can be made more formidable by establishing a higher goal. You may find ones that become favorites or ones that become part of your pre-game ritual. Regardless, it is of the utmost importance to alter the circumstances around your practice even when using these games.

These games assimilate your practice sessions to that of the game of golf and consequently allow your on-course game to excel. These games allow you to, hopefully sooner rather than later, think positively, strategize and hit shots of varying trajectory, roll and curvature. Such skills will develop you into a better player of the game.

Keep a small journal in your golf bag so that you can refer to past practice performances as you strive to better your score and set loftier goals. Some of the games even have a scorecard you can use. If you don't reach your goal at first, don't get discouraged. Know that this type of pressure-packed practice is bettering your game regardless.

> *Confidence comes from being prepared.*
> *-- John Wooden*

While learning the game of golf is an endless path, it is to be enjoyed. It is my hope that the preceding chapters have served as a clearer picture of the importance of competitive practice games. By incorporating the games in the following chapters into your practice sessions, you will understand this necessity and you'll optimize your ability to take it to the course and play better golf. You will have practiced productively and you'll have the tools that will help you to bridge the gap between the practice facility and the golf course.

chapter 7

PUTTING GAMES

There is no similarity between golf and putting; they are two different games – one played in the air, the other on the ground.

— Ben Hogan

STAR

IN A STRAIGHT LINE OUT FROM the hole, place four balls on the green. The first ball should be placed two feet from the hole while the others are positioned further away in one-foot increments making the fourth ball five feet from the hole. This is called an arm. Making four other arms coming out from the hole, as you see in the photo, is what creates a star.

The Star game will provide you with different length putts and also putts that have slight differences in slope and therefore break. The Star game will stimulate your brain as you adapt to the varying length of each putt and the required change in aim as the putt may break more as you move outward on the same arm and definitely as you proceed to a new arm. Short putts in competition and this Star game will test your nerves but that's what it's all about - that's why you're practicing.

GAME #1

Choose one of the arms in which to start. From that arm roll the two-foot ball continuing back to each of the other balls within that arm. Once you've completed the fourth ball in that arm, proceed to a different arm. If you miss a putt along the way, there are a couple of options for you depending on your ability and drive. One would be to start completely over with the first ball from the first arm. Another option would be to just restart from the first ball of the arm that you're currently on. Star is a versatile game because as you reach your goal it can always be made more challenging by adding more golf balls and working your way further from the hole.

GAME #2

This time begin by putting all of the two-foot putts and move outward to the three-foot golf balls and so on. See how far you can go by making consecutive putts. Once you miss, set them up again and strive to get further along than the time before. Remember that recording your best score, meaning how far you went before missing, in a game improvement journal will create an internal drive to improve upon during your next practice session.

Narrow Your Focus

Using a golf tee or a coin and one golf ball, putt as many times as you'd like to this smaller than normal object

Let the ball roll into the tee or over the coin at a speed conducive to gravity pulling it into the hole if you had been putting to one. The point to this game is very psychological. A field goal kicker sometimes practices by booting footballs through field goal posts that are narrower than would be found in a game situation. By practicing to something smaller and more challenging than a regulation sized hole, the golfer, when actually participating in a round of golf, sees the true cup as enormous.

Game #1

Practice putting to a tee striving to contact the tee as the ball rolls to it. You can do the same with a quarter and even on your carpet at home. Another tool I'd recommend is a device that fits over a regulation sized cup that has a smaller hole in the middle to putt into. This device has two sizes. In the photo, we've left the smaller ring out which would make the hole even smaller. Additionally, just like the superintendent cuts the cups in the morning with the regulation diameter of 4 1/4 inches, there is a cup cutting device that is only a couple inches in diameter. See if the superintendent is willing to cut a few of these smaller holes into the practice green each morning. It would be advantageous to roll a few putts at that smaller hole just before teeing off.

Game #2

With a friend, equally toss out a few quarters each on the putting green. Roll your putt as close to the quarter as possible. The person whose ball comes to rest closest to the quarter regardless of whether it rolled over it or came up short, gets the quarter. Proceed on to the other quarters with the same rules. You can play with as many or as few people as you'd like.

PUTTING GAMES 35

Compass

The points in which you will be putting from represent an eight point compass. There are four outer points and four inner ones. The setup should resemble what you see in the photo with the outer balls about four feet and the inner balls at two feet.

There is an important point to having four outer ones mixed with four inner points. Have you ever hit a putt that ended up just a foot or two away from the hole and walked up to quickly knock it in only to have missed it? Sometimes this is true because you failed to go through your routine maybe missing some cue along the way that would have helped you make it. Nonetheless, switching up the distances of your putts engages your brain and doesn't make it monotonous.

Game

Proceed by alternating between a four-foot putt and a two-foot putt striving to complete each point of the compass. Further explanation can be used by using the compass illustrated at the bottom of the photo. Start with the North ball, proceeding to the NW ball, then the West ball, and so on making every putt along the way. If you miss, you must reset all of the balls and start again from the beginning.

You can use this game in several different ways to test your skills:
- *See how many attempts it takes you to complete the compass without missing a single putt.*
- *Given a certain amount of time dedicated to this short putt practice, count the number of times you can successfully complete the compass without missing.*

When your putts from this distance become automatic, change the distance of each ball. Maybe move the outer golf balls to six feet and the inner ones to three.

PUTTING GAMES 37

In A Row

Pick a spot near a hole on your practice putting green that is within six or eight feet of the cup. The putt you choose can be straight or have a curve to it.

This is a competitive game that most kids play from the onset of their practice. They learn to challenge themselves and like almost every game in this book, you can begin from a starting point that matches your ability and make it more challenging as you progress.

The goal is to consecutively roll in a certain number of putts determined before you begin. While you do not get multiple tries on the golf course, this game does create an environment filled with pressure. Thriving under pressure is what will separate you from other players. Practicing in this condition will feed your on-course intensity and desire to make every putt. Many people have told me that making tons of these putts in practice brings them confidence on the course. Tiger Woods uses this game quite often as it provides an abundance of great pictures of the ball going in which can be drawn upon during a competitive round.

Game #1

Simply drop several golf balls on the green at say, four feet and make, depending on your ability ten, twenty, fifty, or one hundred in a row.

Game #2

You can also utilize this game each time you practice by coming out and seeing how many in a row you can make from a designated distance. For example on Monday, you make thirteen in a row. Next time you practice the goal would be to better your score from Monday.

Game #3

Somewhere within six feet of the hole you and a friend compete to see who makes ten in a row in the least number of attempts. An attempt is defined in the following way: Let's say you make your first six putts in a row and miss on your seventh putt. This would constitute one attempt. You then start over again from one trying to make ten in a row. This would be your second attempt. Remember that it is not a race but a test of nerves, perseverance, determination and commitment to your routine. Alternate hitting putts if you find yourself getting too quick.

Spelling

The spelling game is directed at golf teams. It is a form of In A Row but is to be played by the entire golf team. It is a great way for the team to come together, root each other on and at the same time feel a great amount of pressure. Each person who putts puts the weight of the team on his or her shoulders. The pressure comes because the team cannot be dismissed from practice until they've accomplished the goal.

Game

The players on the team pick a word to spell which has as many letters as there are players. It can be a word that describes the type of performance they're looking to have in their next tournament like *win* or *repeat*. The word can describe the attitude the coach is trying to instill in each player like *pride*. It can also be something that relates to the team mascot.

After the team chooses a word that has as many letters as there are players, they line up near the hole at around four feet. Each person putts one at a time and must make their putt. Each consecutive putt made counts as a letter toward spelling the chosen word. Whether the person makes it or misses, he or she must go to the end of the line. If someone misses, the team must start over again with the first letter of the word and the next person in line starts it. If a person does miss and the spelling starts over again with everyone successfully making their putts, it will eventually come to the player who missed the previous time. That person will have to carry the load of the team and be faced with spelling the last letter of the word.

PUTTING GAMES 41

Spiral

BEGINNING FROM ONE FOOT AWAY, spiral out from the hole a total of sixteen or so golf balls.

The benefit of this game comes with not only experiencing putts of different distances but also working around the hole. This will give you a chance to experience different breaking putts as long as you choose a hole with a slight slope to it. A golfer's green reading ability will intensify by paying attention to the slope of each putt, by focusing on the speed and curvature of its roll and by evaluating and learning from the result. Having a purpose to your practice is vital and will relate to the speed in which you learn.

Game #1

Simply see how many in a row you can make. Record that number in your mind or in a journal. Set the balls up again in the same fashion and strive to surpass your last attempt.

Game #2

Before starting, allow yourself a certain number of missed putts. For example, maybe you want to allow yourself five misses. Strive to finish the last ball while staying within your stated number of misses. If not, you must start over.

Game #3

Hit all sixteen putts and see how many you make. Record that number in your journal and try to better it the next time you play this game.

Clock

THIS IS A GAME TO BE USED to gain some confidence from short distances around the hole. It is a beneficial drill to perform just before teeing off.

Clock signifies what will be experienced on the golf course - putts of varying length and curvature with some pressure to succeed. Find a couple of games in this book that bring you confidence and instill them into your pre-game ritual.

Game

Following the photo will help you understand the game. From the 12 o'clock position make 12 putts from two feet. From the 9 o'clock position make 9 putts from three feet. From the 6 o'clock position make 6 putts from four feet and from the 3 o'clock position make 3 putts from five feet. If you made every single putt you would have rolled thirty putts. You can see how many putts it takes you to complete the clock knowing that thirty is a perfect score. A more difficult version is that you must make the putts in a row or you have to start over.

PUTTING GAMES

Random

This is a game for those that don't have a specific place for each club in their bag, but instead have the personality of just shoving them in wherever.

When we play we tend to come upon putts of varying length. This game will move you around the hole putting balls from different locations and lengths.

Game

Standing near to the hole, throw five balls up into the air and begin to putt them from wherever they land. For those more organized people that do have a certain place for each club in their bag, simply place a ball at five feet, a couple of them at four feet, and a couple at three feet. You must make all five in a row or you start over. If you make all five in a row, scatter the balls again and continue to keep your streak alive.

You will usually find holes on a practice putting green that are more sloped or flatter than others. As you make all five in a row, move to one of those holes that has a more challenging slope to it.

PUTTING GAMES 47

Soda Pop Putting

Most putting cups found on practice greens are half the depth of normal cups you'll find on the golf course. These shallow cups work perfect for this game. Begin by placing a juice can or soda can in the hole. As it rests in the cup, the upper portion of the can should rise above the top of the hole.

With the pressures of trying to make the ball drop into a hole out of your mind, this game really promotes focusing on proper speed and is a fabulous game for anyone who is struggling with getting the ball to the hole.

Game

After placing the can in the cup, drop several golf balls and putt toward it. You can start from a distance inside of six feet and move out as you progress. The soda can is smaller than the cup so your focus narrows slightly and then when the can isn't there it tricks the mind into thinking the hole looks bigger. When the can is there, your goal is to bump the ball into the can. It works particularly well for people who constantly leave the ball short of the hole. It's no fun if it doesn't get there.

You can set up a ladder, starting at three feet, then six feet, nine feet and so on. Don't move back until you've hit the can at the proper speed. The can changes your intention and attention. Consequently your stroke may become more definitive and less tentative or guiding. You'll put an exclamation mark to the end of your stroke instead of a stroke that is unsure. This is also a fun game for young juniors.

PUTTING GAMES 49

Tee-Ball

The more precise your touch and feel for the speed of the putting greens is the better. This challenging game will hone your feel, test your ability to focus and refocus.

Your intent is to roll each putt to the chosen tee without hitting it too far or too short. See how far away your target is and stick with your intention.

Game

Place about seven tees in the green, in a straight line and two feet apart. Putt from a distance of around ten feet and begin by aiming for the second tee. Your putt should hit the tee or come to rest, distance wise, between the first and third tees. After succeeding proceed to the third tee. As you intend to roll the ball into that tee, should it not hit the tee, it should stop between the tee before it and after it which in this case would be the second and fourth tees. Continue until you've completed the second to last tee in the group. You can always move closer if you're struggling and further away as you succeed.

Using one ball will make you go through your routine, focus more effectively and consequently become a more disciplined putter. Having to retrieve it for yourself just makes one want to do it right the first time. This is often true on the golf course as well. People hurry through their routine and in doing so hit the ball more often. This will take more time in total than if you had taken more time to evaluate the putt or shot because you'll hit it fewer times over the course of the hole and through the entirety of the round. The time to hurry in golf is between shots not in preparation of or during a shot.

PUTTING GAMES 51

Aces

THE GAME ACES IS ABOUT making the putt. Nothing but a holed putt will suffice as you and an opponent stand opposite each other on the putting green and compete against one another.

It breeds holing putts instead of lagging them. It's a contest to see who can make more putts. If you've found yourself to be timid when trying to hole putts, a contest like this game may be just what you need.

Game

With another person find two holes on the putting green that are between ten and twenty feet part. Each person should be positioned at his own hole with one ball. Both players putt simultaneously to each others hole. Any putt that is holed is worth one point. You should predetermine a point goal to play to. If that number is ten, the first one to reach ten points is declared the winner.

After each person rolls a putt, each person should gather the other person's putt and get ready to putt again simultaneously. Going through your routine will make the environment seem as meaningful as playing on the course and it should help you play with the pressure more effectively.

Make this game more challenging by choosing holes that are farther away or by setting a higher point goal. You can change holes once someone makes one or you can even move close and use smaller holes.

You can play with more people as well. With three people, choose three holes that make up a triangle. Each putt should be relatively similar in distance to the others. Proceed in the same way by putting simultaneously.

PUTTING GAMES 53

Ladder

DO YOU REMEMBER THE LAST TIME you had a great opportunity to make birdie after hitting your approach shot close only to have three-putted and ended up with a bogey? A deflating feeling can overcome you consequently interrupting the positive flow you received from knocking it close.

While practicing putts of all lengths is important, this Ladder game focuses on your feel from inside fifteen feet so that you can increase your chances of making that putt for birdie or walk away with an easy two-putt.

Game #1

Place a tee in the ground at three feet, six feet, nine feet, twelve feet and fifteen feet. The goal is to make the 15-footer without having missed any prior putts. Use one ball and start at three feet progressing further back each time you make one. For instance, if you make the 3-footer, move to the 6-footer. If you make it, move on to the 9-footer and so on. If you miss at any of the distances then you must start over from the 3-foot putt. Each time you putt from the 3-foot tee you are starting a new attempt at trying to complete the ladder. See how many attempts it takes you until you drain the 15-foot putt.

Game #2

Start by using four golf balls. With this game you allow yourself some misses depending on your ability. For example, from three feet you must make all four putts. Once attained, move back to the six foot tee where you will need to make 3 out of the 4 putts; perhaps your goal is 2 out of 4 from nine feet, 2 out of 4 from twelve feet and 1 out of 4 from fifteen feet. It is up to you to alter the number of misses you want to allow yourself. Set the number tough enough though so that you're always striving for improvement and challenging yourself each day.

Ladder With Border

PLACE THE FLAGSTICK OR A CLUB two feet behind the hole. Then place five tees in the ground. One each at three feet, six feet, nine feet, twelve feet and fifteen feet.

While the ultimate goal is always for the ball to roll into the hole, if it doesn't come to rest in the bottom of the cup it should stop beyond the front edge of the cup, illustrated by the dashed line in the photo, and yet short of the club behind the hole.

This game will make your putting touch more acute by zoning in on your "area of allowed miss." By striving to get it past the hole, you're giving it a chance to go in yet at the same time, setting a barrier behind the hole so that you still keep each ball within a reasonable distance from the cup. This will make for an easy tap-in if you don't happen to drain it.

Game #1

Using four golf balls, start from three feet. Set some parameters for yourself. For example, from three feet and six feet, all four putts must comply with the rules. From nine feet and twelve feet, 3 out of 4 and from fifteen feet, 2 out of 4 must comply or you will need to start over again from the three-foot tee. Of course, you should set those parameters based on your level of play and improve each time you practice.

Game #2

With this version, you will only be allowed to use one golf ball. The rules are the same yet your goal is to complete the fifteen-footer having started from the three foot tee. As long as your putt complies with the rules, you may move back. If it doesn't, you must start over at the three-foot tee. Each time you putt from the three-foot tee counts as an attempt. Record how many attempts it takes to successfully complete the fifteen-foot putt.

PUTTING GAMES 57

Shotgun

Shotgun is a game that can be played by yourself, against a friend or with your golf team. Using as many holes as there are players, place five balls at each hole. At one of the holes, position all five balls three feet from the cup. You can pile the balls in one location but setting them around the hole in a circle will change the break for each attempt and make it more realistic. At another hole, place five more balls six feet away. Continue placing five balls at each of the additional holes in increments of three feet. For instance, the next hole will have golf balls that are nine feet away. Another should be encircled with balls that are twelve feet away, then fifteen feet away, etc. As you can see in the photo, with this team of three, they've positioned themselves at three, six and nine feet.

Game

In a team atmosphere, shotgun start everyone at their own hole. Each team member putts their five golf balls and after doing so moves in accordance to a different hole. Continue until every hole has been completed. With the example in the photo, each team member will have rolled fifteen putts. See how many out of those fifteen each player sinks and challenge each other to see who makes the most putts.

If you're practicing by yourself, set a certain number of distances that will need to be completed. For example putt five balls each from three, six, nine, twelve and fifteen feet. Having rolled twenty-five putts, see how many you make and document the number made from each distance.

PUTTING GAMES 59

The Need for Speed

This game has nothing to do with quickness but everything to do with controlling the speed and therefore distance of your medium to long putts. In golf you've got to be proficient with the flatstick. And while three-putting is inevitable, the better you are at long putts and short putts the less you'll walk off the green having taken three putts.

Game

If you can't find a hole on the putting green that is cut two feet from the fringe, place a cut out circle of a hole or a tee two feet from the edge of the fringe. From ten to twenty feet, the ball must go past the front edge of the hole (designated by the string in the photo) but short of the fringe. From thirty and forty feet, move the string a foot or so in front of the hole and again, get the ball to stop between the string and the fringe. Though string is not necessary for this game it can easily settle any disputes. A number of golfers enjoy using a chalk line to practice their putting stroke. If you have one, you can substitute it for the string.

Remember that the ultimate goal is to make the putt, so pick your line, stay decisive and sense the speed. Using one ball will always make it feel more realistic. To add a dash of pressure challenge a friend or keep track yourself by adding up the number of putts, out of ten, that you successfully make from each distance. This is also a wonderful game for an entire golf team to play. Set up the string and hole. Line up the team and putt one at a time. The team is not dismissed from practice until everyone consecutively rolls their ball between the string and fringe.

In-Between

PLACE TWO TEES TEN FEET APART on the practice putting green or a couple of quarters at home on your carpet. In the photo, you'll see string being used as the border.

The goal is to get as many balls in between these two objects. Being able to control the distance that you hit your putts is crucial to your putting success. You will constantly hear tour pros and teaching professionals advocate speed control. This game can develop your feel in the finest of degrees.

Game #1

Working your way from short to long, try to get your ball past the first string but short of the second string. Challenge yourself by seeing how many balls you can get between the strings while progressively increasing your distance with each putt.

When you challenge a friend you can follow this scenario. If Player A goes first and gets four balls within the strings while abiding by the progressively longer rule, Player A, on his fifth attempt, can choose to go ahead with his fifth attempt or pass. By passing, he is challenging Player B to try to get more than four balls In-Between. Player A should remove his golf balls and let Player B play away.

You can also progressively work your way from long to short as shown in the photo. In this case you'd want to hit your first putt as close to the furthest border object as possible and work your way back toward you.

Game #2

Set the strings up using the 10% rule, which means if you're 20-feet away your ball should end up two feet away from the hole if it doesn't go in. If you're 30-feet away your ball should end up three feet away. If you're 40-feet away your putt should end up within four feet of the hole, et cetera.

So let's say you choose to work on your 30-footers. Set the strings six feet apart. With an imaginary hole located directly in between the strings, ten percent of thirty leaves you three feet short of the hole and three feet beyond it. See how many putts in a row you can allow to come to rest in between the strings. Change distances often and journal your scores for future use.

3x3

FIND A RELATIVELY FLAT AREA on the putting green. As you improve, you can challenge yourself by choosing an area that is either slightly uphill or downhill.

The goal is to have each ball come to rest three feet from the previous ball. Play this game several times until you feel comfortable with the speed. Golfers tend to have better touch some days compared to others. Performing this exercise before you play will increase your chances of having proper feel on the greens that day.

By developing the fine feel for how much the putter actually swings more or less to get the ball to end up three feet further or shorter than the previous ball will give you a touch which will make your opponents envious. Precise distance control will ultimately assist in making more putts while avoiding the dreaded three-putt.

Game #1

Using five golf balls, hit the first putt fifteen to twenty feet. Now hit your second one letting it stop three feet short of the first putt. Regardless of where the previous putt came to rest, strive to hit your third putt three feet short of it. Proceed with the fourth and fifth balls. Walk to the side of this line and check the distance between each ball. On a rainy day, you can even do this inside on your carpet. While the carpet may produce a slightly different pace to your putts than the greens on your home course, being able to adapt and feel what three feet is within your putting stroke will give you an edge on the dance floor.

Game #2

Using five golf balls, hit the first one three to five feet in front of you. Move your aim over slightly so as to avoid hitting the first ball and roll your second ball three feet past it. No matter where your second putt comes to rest, hit your third putt three feet past it. Continue with the fourth then fifth putt. Step to the side of this line of balls to check the ball dispersion. Because the length of most putters is between 33" and 35" they make for an easy measuring tool if you don't want to eyeball your results.

Fringe Benefits

FIND A PLACE ON THE GREEN that is open enough that it gives you a direct route to the fringe. Start from approximately fifteen feet away. You can move further away as you improve but don't ever feel ashamed to move closer if you're struggling. After all, you experience putts of different lengths each time you set foot on the putting green during a round of golf. Practicing putts that vary in distance resembles what you'll encounter when you play so start as close as you'd like.

The goal is to roll each putt with the intent of having it come to rest against the edge of the fringe and the putting surface. In putting, having the touch to control the distance that the ball travels is crucial. This game will help develop your speed control creating a deft touch for any length putt.

Game #1

Using a few golf balls, putt each one toward the edge of the fringe. Look how you've done after each putt and better the result with each putt you roll. While you don't get multiple tries when you play, this is a beginning point to developing your feel as long as you stay aware of your body and your feel. You can speed your learning by being specific in your observation of each putt. Watch each ball. See how it rolls and at what speed. Blend what you see with what you felt in order to improve the next one.

Fringe Benefits (continued)

Game #2

This time you will actually look at the edge of the fringe as you stroke the putt. That's right - do not look at the ball while stroking it. You'll be surprised after several rounds how good you are without having to look at the ball. If this concept sounds strange to you, remind yourself that the ball is not moving and then think about how many other sports you play while looking at the target while performing the swing, throw, shot, or other action. Take on a friend if you'd like and see who can get it closer.

Game #3

In this version you will address the ball, look at the fringe to give your brain a picture of how far away you are, look back at the ball, close your eyes, and with your eyes still closed roll it to the edge. Feel free to take practice swings if you wish, just make sure that your eyes stay closed during the actual stroke. Why you ask? Many great putters have long admitted that they don't look at a specific part of the ball when addressing or putting the ball. Instead, they see a snapshot of the grass, the slope and the hole just as if they were really looking at it. Their eyes are more in a trance while their mind's eye sees the track or line that the ball will take. After all, the ball won't give you any important information required to make the putt. Closing your eyes can help you envision the trail or line and the pace the ball will have as gravity takes it to the bottom of the cup.

Pitching Quarters

Find an open place on the practice putting green where you and a partner can roll putts of varying distance to the edge of the fringe. If a line to the fringe isn't accessible, find a place on the green that is and lay down some string in that area.

Strive to roll each putt with the intent of having it come to rest as close as possible to that string or fringe. It can roll past it or come up short. Just get it close. In other cases you can alter that rule. For instance, roll each putt toward the string or fringe but it cannot go past it or set the rule that it cannot end up short.

You will increase your ability to control the distance that your putts travel and at the same time gain valuable experience in feeling the pressure of competing against another person. Additionally, it can be psychologically important to practice putting without the use of a hole.

Game #1

If you've ever pitched quarters using coins against a friend, you know that the goal is to get the quarter to end up closer to the wall than your opponent. The same holds true with this game. With one ball each, challenge one another from different distances and see who can roll it the closest to the object. With the coin game, the winner actually gets the loser's quarter. Golf balls these days cost a lot more than a quarter but you can decide the wager.

Game #2

With three golf balls each, roll your putts toward the object. With a tape measure, total up the distance your three golf balls came to rest from the object and compare that to the total distance of your opponent's three balls. Whoever has a smaller total is the winner. This game really keeps your focus on each putt. Just because you think you may have "messed up" on one of your putts doesn't mean that it's over. Never give up. Perseverance is a character trait in which the game of golf will reward.

10 - 20 - 30 - 40

FIND A PLACE ON THE PRACTICE putting green that will allow you enough space to hit putts of forty feet. Place a tee in the ground at 10 feet, 20 feet, 30 feet and 40 feet. In the photo, we replaced tees with disks just to make them easier to see.

The goal is to cozy each ball up next to or parallel to the tee that you're putting toward. Obviously, the closer the better, but you be the judge on what is acceptable based on your ability.

Strictly a game to improve your touch for lengthier putts, this game will help you develop a better feel for rolling the ball closer to the hole and hence giving it a better chance to drop. Whether you pitched it onto the green or hit another green in regulation, you'll find yourself outside of ten feet quite often and need to walk off the green with having no more than two putts. The PGA Tour average is 1.6 putts per hole.

Game #1

Hit all four putts to the 10-foot tee. Once you feel you've succeeded in your attempts at the goal, gather up the balls and putt the four balls to the 20-foot tee. Continue until you've completed the putts of 30 and 40 feet. Remember that it's not a race, but an exercise to increase your ability to control the distance that you roll your putts. You can replay the game starting with the 40-foot tee and work your way closer to you. Feel free to set up parameters for yourself allowing some leeway for missing a little long or short of the tee.

Game #2

Alternate your target for each ball that you roll. For example, start by putting one ball to the 30-footer. Roll one ball to the 10-foot tee, then the 40-foot tee and finally to the 20-foot tee. If any of those putts are outside of the parameter of acceptance that you set, start over again. After a successful run at all four distances, begin again but change up the order of the tees you putt to. A friend or curious onlooker is sure to show up and a friendly competition is on.

PUTTING GAMES 73

The Track

There is a track on every putting green just waiting to be run. While it's not a race for time, it is a race to see who can putt the course in the fewest number of strokes. The course needs no setup as it's already there to be put to the test.

Simply putt around the outer holes of the putting green in the fewest number of putts without straying from the course as described below.

Game

Start by placing two tees in the ground anywhere on the edge of the putting green. You will begin your first putt from there. Each putt must stay on the outer side of those holes without touching the fringe. If you stray from the course, either by putting inside the holes or outside of the fringe, then a one stroke penalty must be incurred and you must place your ball at the point in which it crossed the boundary.

The person whose ball passes through the two tees in the fewest number of strokes is the winner. You can change the course by starting from a different location or by changing one of the holes and therefore altering the track. There is a number to every course that you will not be able to go lower than so change the course once you've reached that number. At respectable golf courses the practice putting cups will be changed quite frequently, hopefully every few days, so the course will automatically change for you.

Eyes Closed

By closing your eyes, your mind tends to clean itself out of all of the extraneous jargon that you tend to cultivate when over a shot or putt. Instead, the brain begins to "see" a picture of your goal, the hole. It can be as simple as that … there it is, roll it there. After you close your eyes, either consciously or subconsciously, your brain remembers how far away the hole is, what the grass looks like, and the slope of the green. This frees up your body to perform better and you become more aware. You will make a more decisive stroke, seeing only what is necessary and not any extra information that is worthless and distractive. Without proper direction and consistency to your mental routine, it is easy to second guess yourself while over a putt. Seeing the line, sensing the pace, or seeing it drop into the cup in your mind's eye before you actually hit the putt, is what is called process goals. If you do all that you can preparatory wise, you will be increasing the likelihood that the putt will drop. Then you simply need to carry that process to every putt you have. Consistency to your results begins with the consistency of your routine.

Game

Start about fifteen feet away from the hole. You can look at the hole as many times as you wish but just before you hit it, close your eyes. Hit the putt and see how you've done. It may take a few attempts until your results become acceptable, but remember the purpose is to bring to the forefront your innate ability to control the distance of your putts by getting out of your own way.

Variations

One additional aspect you can incorporate into this game is to guess at the result before you open your eyes. So again, with your eyes closed, roll the putt but this time before you open them, take a guess based on your feel, as to if the ball ended up too long, too short, or within an acceptable distance away from the hole. As you practice and improve your touch, you should be able to roll each putt within an acceptable distance and still be able to say if it was a little long or short of the hole

- that's exceptional feel. You may remember Michael Jordan shooting free throws during an actual game with his eyes closed. This is the same thing. The hoop or hole in this case isn't going to move. You're not going to whiff the putt. Closing your eyes will bring out that inherent ability within you to refine your feel.

Twenty-One

Twenty-one is a game that you can compete against a large number of players or just one opponent. It is quite popular among tour pros, junior golfers and golf teams.

Game

You can use a single hole that is down sloping, one that is uphill, a big breaker or switch to different holes on the putting green like a course. Each player putts one ball to the hole from the same location. The first player to twenty-one points is the winner. Players receive two points for a make, one point if it misses but goes past the hole and a negative point for any putt that ends up short. This is a great game if you or any player on the team has been struggling to get the ball to the hole.

You can also play this game by yourself. Instead of competing against someone else for score, you'll be competing against your own ability by simply counting the number of holes it takes you to reach twenty-one points. The fewer number of holes the better. Don't forget to record that number in your game improvement journal so that you can remember what your record is with the intent of beating it the next time you practice.

Two Ball Game

CHALLENGE A FRIEND OR PLAY against yourself. All that you will need is two golf balls each, the ability to forget a poor shot by finding pleasure in the next one and a desire for what is often called the game within the game … putting.

I seldom advocate using two balls simply because people always choose the better ball and go from there. Typically this happens because the first ball was not up to their expectations but the true game of golf is about the first and only ball. Consequently, you receive a false sense of score so when you actually play by the rules, without mulligans for instance, you find yourself getting upset with a poor result and taking that attitude into your next shot and you're doomed to repeat the process all over again. Not a fun way to play golf.

The only time a second ball is worthy is if you're in a practice round learning the course. If you hit a poor shot, the result is not what matters, your ability to forget it, go on with your next shot wherever it may be is. I find myself telling junior golfers the following and I think adults can certainly benefit from this just as much:

> *Golf is about many things, honesty, integrity, and friendship to name a few, but it's also about how you react and recover when the ball doesn't go where you had intended.*

How do you react? This Two Ball game will help develop the ever so important skill of "letting go." After all, the most important shot in golf is the one you're currently faced with, not the last one or a future one.

Game

With two golf balls, putt both balls to the hole and always choose the worst putt hitting two balls again from that spot, so on and so forth, until both balls are holed. Your first putting location should be of sizable distance. If one ball ends up one inch from the hole and the other is four feet short, retrieve the closer ball and hit two putts from the four-foot location. Continuing on, if you make one of those four-footers but roll the other two feet past, retrieve the better ball, which in this case is in the hole, and hit two balls from that two-foot location. You will continue until both balls are holed from the same location. You can also keep score and play against a friend. In the case of our example, if you continued by holing both balls from the two foot location you would have scored a three on that hole. Here' how: The attempt from far away counted as one, the attempt from four feet counted as your second and the holing out of both balls from two feet was your third.

Drawback

DRAWBACK IS SIMILAR TO HAVING a putting contest against a friend or with yourself, except this game has a twist to the rules. While you won't make every putt, you'll come to understand why it's so important to do so.

Drawback promotes one to really focus and strive to make the first putt. But the true reason for the game is to get in short putt practice under pressure. If you miss your first attempt you will always be left with some sort of putt over three feet which golfers tend to have numerous putts of that length throughout the course of a round.

Game

Whether you have a contest with yourself or against a friend, with every putt that doesn't go in, you must draw the ball back a putter's length from wherever your ball rests until it is holed. As you'll find out, making three to four-foot putts is crucial in this game for if you leave one on the lip, you still have to draw it back a putter's length and give it another roll. If you need to draw it back make sure you pull it back in line with the center of the hole and the ball.

Play a designated number of holes and see what your stroke total is at the completion of that course. Playing this game by yourself works just as well as playing against another person.

PUTTING GAMES 83

Sevens

This putting game is quite popular around our teaching center. Grab a buddy to play and while it takes at least two to play, you can have an endless number of participants. This game resembles good putting. It will promote you to never give up. It will reward those putts that are holed and it will train the proper speed of each putt so if missed it sits within tap-in distance. And just like the entire game of golf, this putting game breeds competitiveness with the enjoyment of others.

By accumulating points, in a fashion described below, the first one to seven points wins.

Game

A toss of a coin or flip of a tee will determine who picks the first hole and putts first. Here's how you accumulate points:

- *If you hole out in one stroke you get 2 points*
- *If no one holes out in their first attempt, the person whose ball comes to rest closest to the hole gains 1 point*
- *Everyone must then continue by putting out. If you hole out in a total two strokes, you receive 0 points and if you three putt, you subtract a point from your score.*

Scoring

Holed out in one stroke   = 2 points
Closest to the hole   = 1 point
Three putt or worse   = -1 point

VARIATIONS

If you wish, you can apply any of the following rules to Sevens. Just be sure that the rules are clear before you start as everyone has slight variations to the game.

- *You can allow for stymies*
- *If no one holes out on their first putt, the person whose ball lies closest to the hole without being short receives the one point.*
- *For the game to be completed the winner must end exactly with seven points otherwise he or she starts over with zero points.*
- *If a person holes their first putt receiving two points but someone else tops it, the second person also receives two points.*

Putting Contest

If you're lucky enough to have an actual putting course near your home they can be a lot of fun. There aren't too many around the country so your local practice putting green is more than sufficient.

Putting contests evoke pressure packed situations. Therefore they are a fitting way to gain more experience feeling the pressure and testing your routine and focus for the process.

I was lucky to grow up on a golf course in Colorado called Hyland Hills. For one, it consisted of two par 3 courses one of which was very flat and hazardless while the other was the opposite. Growing up as a junior golfer I could then progress to the regulation length 9-hole course and finally to the championship 18-hole course. I was also lucky because I met a lot of juniors my age there. Many of us began working there and ended up as professionals at other clubs. One of my fondest memories was having putting contests with a bunch of guys. They lasted so long that we would see a group tee off on the first hole and finish the eighteenth. I knew I was doing something great for my game by participating in those putting contests and it is that memory that inspired me to compile these games and publish them into this book.

Game #1

Play nine or eighteen holes against a friend or with a group of friends. Choose either stroke play or match play. If you don't know the difference between the two, here's an example: On hole #1 it takes Player A two putts to get the ball in the hole, while it takes Player B four putts to hole out. In stroke play, Player A is up by a total of two strokes. Match play is simply determined by who wins each hole. So in our example, Player A would be up by one hole.

Game #2

You can have a stroke play contest with yourself. Start by determining how many holes you are going to play. You can either set a goal for yourself as far as the number of strokes you want to complete the course in before you can go home or a more basic version would be to simply see how many putts it takes you to complete your course. With the latter, you should record that score in your mind or in a practice journal and try to better your score each time you practice. In the first version of Game #2, you'll feel the pressure building as you near the last few holes close to your stated goal. Stay with your routine just as you should on the golf course. It is just another putt that you've made hundreds if not thousands of times before.

Can't Leave Until...

This is an all-encompassing game that works for many of the putting games described in the pages prior to this one. Can't Leave Until is exactly what it sounds like. You must fill in the rest of the sentence with a challenge of your own.

One of the most important things I was ever told was that your body can still perform extremely well if you're nervous, shaky, or feeling the pressure. This is only true if your mind is at ease and you're focused on your intention. You can feel the heat of the moment even be a little shaky as long as your thinking isn't over technical or negative.

As do many of the games in this book, this game reveals your character under pressure. You can learn to curb your frustration and thrive under pressure simply by inviting yourself into and enjoy being in a pressure situation. Consequently, you'll become the player you want to become. You'll make more putts under the gun and beat your buddies most every time.

Game #1

Let's say you're playing 9-holes on the putting green. As always this depends on your ability but say your goal is to two-putt all 9-holes. So as the game states, you Can't Leave Until you two-putt every hole during one round. You'll feel the pressure build as you get to the 7th, then 8th, and finally the 9th hole. Back away if you need to as it's not a race. Go through your routine, stay confident, see it going in if you're visual, definitely know that it's going in and let it go.

Game #2

One version that you may have already thought of would be to make twenty putts in a row from a certain distance and yes, you Can't Leave Until you do. Again, you'll feel the pressure build as you near your last few attempts. If you can begin to feel yourself under pressure as you hit your 17th, 18th, 19th and 20th putt, tell yourself this is what it's all about. I once taught with a great teacher, Keith Lyford, who played competitively on tour for a time and who teaches today in California. During his playing days, he held true to his word and it took him eight hours to complete his consecutive one hundred in a row goal. How dedicated and determined are you?

chapter 8

CHIPPING GAMES

Improve your chipping and you automatically improve your scoring.

-- Tom Watson

Cricket

This game is taken from the dart game by the same name. In darts you must get three 20s before you move on and attempt to get three 19s, then 18s, 17s, 16s, 15s, before ending with three bulls eyes.

With this chipping version of Cricket choose a number of holes of varying length on the chipping green. In this case, we have chosen five holes and placed string in a circle around each hole. The diameter of this circle of string should be based on your ability and what you consider to be an acceptable chip shot.

Game #1

In this game of Cricket you will need an opponent. Each player hits three consecutive shots to the first hole. Once you have hit your three then your opponent hits three consecutive shots to the first hole. Once a player gets three balls in the circle he or she then moves on to the second chosen hole. If for instance, on Player A's first attempt at the first hole he gets two out of three balls into the circle, Player B then goes and after Player B hits three shots Player A still must get one more ball into the circle on hole #1 before proceeding on to hole #2. Keep in mind that each player only gets to hit three shots at a time. The first player to complete the entire course by getting three balls within each circle is the winner.

Game #2

Version two consists of practicing the same game alone instead of with an opponent. Again you must have three chips come to rest in the circle of the first hole before moving on to hole #2. Here you simply count the total number of chips that it takes you to complete the entire course that you've set up.

Another single player variation is to use six golf balls; three balls with the same manufacturer's number (perhaps they're all number 1s) while the other three have a different number (say 4s). Act as two people using the same rule base. See which ball number wins the game.

Inside and Out

Place a couple of tees in the green with one being three feet after the hole and the other three feet before the hole. You can also use string to create these two borders as shown in the photo. If you find the border objects to be distracting, use a club as a measuring device to check if after each shot the ball fell within your boundary. *Note: most putters fall between 34-35 inches in length and your driver is likely around 43-45 inches.* Feel free to widen the border you created if it seems too tough but the long term goal is to eventually shrink the border and hence your misses.

The goal when playing is to gain as many points as possible by holing every chip or by getting it inside the designated border. The point system is described in Game #1 and the rules below state using multiple balls but it is not necessary; you're welcome to use less than what has been suggested. It can be more difficult to focus on hitting multiple balls than it is to concentrate for a short amount of time on one ball like when you're playing. It is for this reason that if you can focus on hitting, say five balls, then the one on the course just became easier. Just be extremely aware of when you've lost your focus. If you sense that you have, reduce the number of balls you're using.

Game #1

After you've designated a border, chip a series of five balls giving yourself two points if you hole the chip, one point if it fails to drop but comes to rest inside the border and zero if it does not. Set a point goal for yourself before you move out further from the green. For instance, once you accumulate five points out of five balls, move back three paces and try the game again. Only move out further after you've accumulated five points. See how far back you can go.

Game #2

With the same border setup, chip five balls from three paces off the green. Add up your points, as in Game #1 then move back three more paces. Hit those five balls again adding up your points. Then proceed back one more time another three paces. Add up your total points that you accumulated from the three spots and fifteen balls that you hit. Write down that point total and challenge yourself by seeing how high your point total can get. You can easily create a match against a friend with this point system.

Game #3

Against a friend or two, start from three paces off of the green and alternate hitting shots. You accumulate points in the same fashion as in the other two games. Set a designated number of spots around the green, hitting five balls, three balls or just one from each spot. Remember to alternate though. Adding up your total as you go along will add pressure and keep the game exciting as you compete against one another and ultimately yourself.

Measure Up

Similar to a round of golf when low score wins, this game's winner is determined by the lowest total amount of feet, or inches if you're really good, that your chips end up from the hole. Some sort of measuring device will be needed for this game. If a tape measure isn't handy, just put some string in your bag with measurements marked on it.

This game will make evident which clubs you chip well with and in what situations. Of course, this also means that this game will help show which clubs you need to work on. You should take away from both of the versions described below that every ball matters. Don't get lazy, stay focused and get every chip close.

Game #1

Choose three different holes on the chipping green. Try to pick one that is close to you, one that is far away and one that is in between the two. Using one club, chip five balls to each hole. Measure the distance each ball comes to rest from the hole.

Then hit five more balls to each of those same three holes using a different club. Perform this exercise with multiple clubs jotting down your measurements each time. Charting your measurements combined with the club used will exhibit which clubs are better suited for certain distances and situations.

Recording this information (perhaps even averaging the distance that the five balls finish from the hole) at the beginning of the season will give you a reference point for where your chipping game currently stands. Playing this game throughout the season will give you status updates but performing it at the end will give you an inventory of how well your chipping game has progressed. Be sure to take note of how far from each hole you were so you can repeat that distance each time you test yourself.

Game #2

Take on a friend and hit five balls to a chosen hole and see whose total is lower after measuring them. The winner of that hole gets to pick the next hole and from what location the shot will be played from. Predetermine a certain number of holes and then you can decide if you would like to play stroke play which means you will have an ongoing total of your measurements or if you want to play match play in which the person with the lowest measurement total on one particular hole is deemed the winner of that hole.

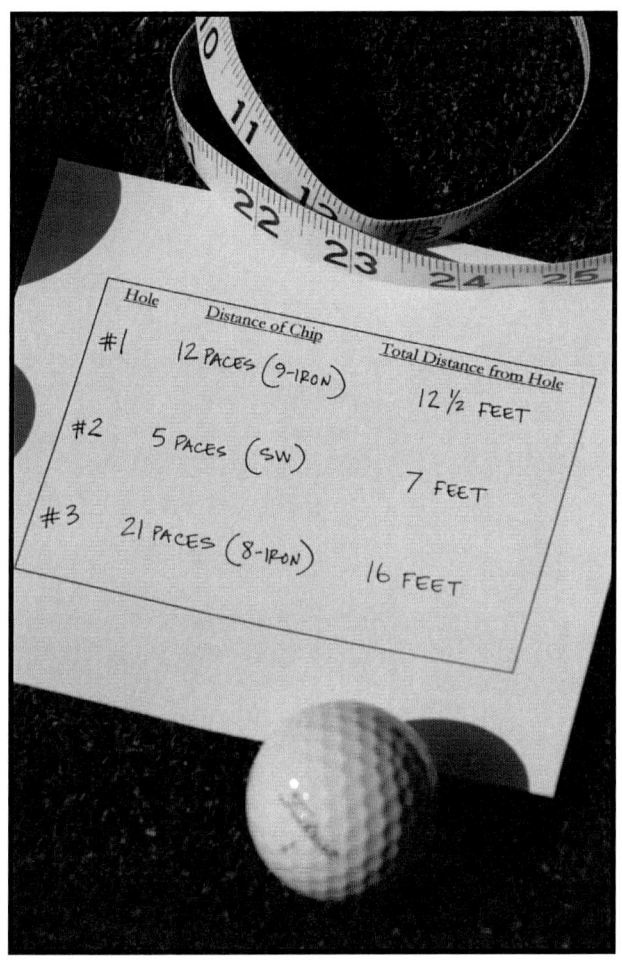

Tee-Ball

Reach in your golf bag and pull out seven tees. Place each tee in the ground at a distance from one another that challenges your ability. A starting point would be to place them in the ground three feet apart. Your goal is to chip each ball as close to the intended tee as possible. This game will narrow your focus and fine tune your touch.

Tee-Ball will hone your distance control by sharpening the minute differences to the length and pace of your chipping motion as well as the trajectory. Your ability to chip it close will be greatly enhanced.

Game

You may use one club for every shot or change clubs - you should use what works best as you strive to hit it as close to the target tee as possible. It's time to zero in and be decisive. You will be chipping to any of the five tees between the first one and the last one. The tees on each end don't have boundaries before or after them respectively so they will never be target tees. The first target tee you should chip toward is actually the second tee in the row. You can proceed on to the next tee once your chip comes to rest not short of the tee in front of the target tee and yet not long of the tee positioned behind the target tee. After you've completed several successful repetitions, reduce the distance between each tee and continue with the same exercise. You can challenge a friend by seeing who gets the closest to each tee or make a game of it alone by counting the number of chips it takes you to successfully complete the five target tees.

Horse

If you grew up shooting hoops, you're very likely to recognize this game. Playing Horse when chipping around the green with a friend is similar to the basketball shooting game played all over the country in parks and in driveways by kids and adults.

The goal is to pick a shot that you can pull off but that you don't think your opponent is capable of topping. In the game Horse, whether it's basketball or golf, one of the fun aspects is that you can change the word you choose to spell. You can spell the word MISSISSIPPI or DOG - it just depends on how much time you have.

Game

An important rule that needs to be set before starting should be to define exactly what a "successful" and "unsuccessful" shot is. One example of how to determine this is that the ball must come to rest within one club length of the hole. That boundary can certainly be changed for every hole but it must be the same for each player and is determined by the first player and before he or she hits. In the photo, the holes are encircled with a valuable practice system consisting of different diameter circles.

In our example we have Players A and B though more can certainly participate. Player A won the coin toss and will go first. If Player A pulls off the chip shot and Player B fails to do so, Player B accumulates a letter. In this case, since "horse" is the word being spelled, Player B would unwelcomingly accumulate the letter "h." If Player B pulls off the shot, then Player A chooses another shot. If Player A is unsuccessful in the attempt, Player B now gets to choose the chip shot of choice and the roles become reversed. The first one to spell the word HORSE is deemed the loser.

CHIPPING GAMES 101

Five Ball Game

I LEARNED THE FULL SWING VERSION of this game from a teacher with whom I used to work. He advocated his students use it with the full swing and then he transformed it into the short game. Merging it into a chipping game with a scoring system will challenge you and put pressure on you. See how many points you can accumulate.

Game

You can use any number of clubs you'd like. For this example, we've chosen a sand wedge, 9-iron and 7-iron. Starting with your sand wedge, hit five balls to a designated hole. Once you've completed the round with those five balls, hit five more with your 9-iron to a different hole and so on accumulating points along the way in the following manner.

+1 point for an acceptable shot
-1 point for an unacceptable shot

With three clubs and hitting five balls with each one this equates to fifteen possible points. What makes the point system challenging is that you subtract a point for a poor result. So if you hit ten acceptable shots and five unacceptable shots your total score would only be five.

Vary the game each time you play by using different clubs or only one club. You can easily play against a friend wagering who carries the other's golf bag back to the car. You may have to place a circle of string around the hole so that there is no dispute over an acceptable or unacceptable result. If string isn't handy, just use a club to check if each shot comes to rest inside its length.

Closest To

GRAB A BALL, YOUR BUDDY and your sticks and take part in probably the most commonly played game that goes on at practice facilities everywhere.

As the game's title states, closest to the hole wins. Remember, nothing can get closer than a ball resting in the bottom of the cup so knock it in but be aware that it better reside close to the hole if it fails to drop.

Game

Challenge a friend to play against. Both players hit a chip to the same hole. The person's ball that comes to rest closest to that hole wins and is allowed to choose the next hole and location from which to chip.

A nice feature to this game is the fact that there can be countless people all competing together. Everybody can throw in a nickel and the person with the most number of "closest to's" after 9-holes wins the pot. If there's a tie, you might as well have a "closest to" chip off.

In a Row

ENCIRCLE A HOLE WITH A STRING, or the Lag Golf System circle as we have in the photo, in a diameter that suits your ability level but yet challenges it at the same time. A general guideline that you can apply to this diameter is the *10% plus 2* rule. This rule means that your ball should get within ten percent of the total distance you are away from the hole plus two feet. For instance, if you're chipping to a hole that is thirty feet away, then a ball that comes to rest within ten percent of that, three feet plus two more feet totaling five is the acceptable diameter. This is just a general guideline. Whether a larger or smaller diameter, you should devise a personal system that calls for the improvement of your skills. Make certain that you reduce the diameter as time goes on.

A chip that doesn't go in the hole should be traveling at a pace that stays close to the hole. The shorter the putt, the greater chance you have of rolling it in.

Game #1

Strive to hit as many chips in a row that come to rest either in the hole or inside the circle. Record this number in a journal yourself or set up a team journal if you belong to a golf team. In this manner, members of the team can compete attempting to better the record over the course of a season.

Game #2

Set a goal for yourself by stating a number, say ten, that must reside inside the designated border in consecutive shots. Increase that goal each time you reach it and see how high your personal best ends up by the end of the season. As you approach that goal, you'll begin to feel pressure similar to what is experienced on the course. You may also get frustrated as you miss time and time again. It may be that frustration that is producing that miss. Be aware and recognize when you're not in the best frame of mind. Resiliency is what turns good players into great players.

Lily Pad Chipping

Locate a spot just a few yards off the green which gives you an angle to chip to three flags of varying distance. This game offers the opportunity to experiment using different clubs which is likely to increase your adaptability and versatility.

Depending on the situation, one example may be that you use a 7-iron to the far pin, a 9-iron to the pin in the middle and a sand wedge to the close hole. If your current chipping method involves primarily using one club and you've never given other clubs a fair chance, then challenge yourself by grabbing a different one. For instance, use an 8-iron to every hole then switch to a pitching wedge. While you may not hit that 8-iron to the hole cut close to you, you should be able to pull the shot off and increase your feel for the shot. The club you choose on the course should be based on the success you've had in practice and your comfort level all the while playing to your strengths.

Game #1

Hit one shot to the close flag, then one to the second flag and finally to the far flag. I believe your goal is to make these types of shots no matter what your ability. If it doesn't go in, whether the result was acceptable or not depends on your ability. One example of an acceptable result is that all shots should get within four feet of the target. A more challenging one could be that you must hole one of the three while the others get within a certain distance. Once you reach your goal, move back a few yards, hit toward different holes, or move to a different location around the green again striving to reach your goal.

Your border around each hole can be designated with string. If you forgot to bring string along, just use one of your clubs as a measuring tool.

Game #2

Hit five balls to the close hole then proceed by putting them in. Set a goal for yourself. Let's say it is to get up-and-down successfully four out of the five balls. After reaching your goal, chip the five balls to the hole in the middle, then finally chip to the far hole reaching your goal at each hole before moving on to the next. Once you complete all three holes in succession, you can start over with the far hole and work your way back. You can pick different holes, or make your goal more challenging.

The realization of this game to golf comes from developing a goal and the pressures that revolve around reaching it. To not set a goal is to just go through the motions which will help you very little if at all when in competition.

On the Mark

Use a quarter, a scorecard or something similar as your landing spot. At our learning center, we use different sized disks cut out of plastic. They have multiple uses but for this game, one will be used as the landing area. Also bring along a friend to help judge your accuracy.

Being a short game wizard requires that you have a plethora of shots that you can call on no matter what the circumstance. This requires an imagination and a deft touch. On The Mark will help you create that touch.

Game

With a friend looking on, hit a chip with your goal being to hit the disk on a fly. A major component to this game is that you cannot watch the ball in flight. I would suggest that you hit the shot with your eyes open and close them as the ball leaves the clubface. Before you open your eyes, your job is to guess whether the ball landed too short, too long or within an acceptable distance of the disk. You and your friend decide what area around the disk makes up this acceptable distance. After you open your eyes, have your friend touch the exact point in which your ball landed, even if your guess was correct. You need that feedback so that you can alter your next shot, if needed. Continue this game for ten golf balls before switching. As you continue you should realize an increased awareness of your feel for the contact and the length and pace of the swing. If you get really good you'll know it's acceptable when you hear the ball land directly on the mark.

Helpful aids may be visualizing the shot or taking practice swings rehearsing the exact length and pace to the swing that you'll need for the shot in front of you. I would strongly suggest that you also have a hole that the ball should be rolling to. While this game helps increase your feel awareness, your brain and body need desperately to know what the final goal is and when you chip, that would be the hole. Don't get consumed solely by the landing spot. Expand your attention to the remainder of the picture which is the ball rolling out to the cup.

CHIPPING GAMES 111

In-Between

Position a couple of tees, or string as you can see in the photo, fifteen feet apart on the practice green. Strive to get as many chips to come to rest between the two objects and yet with some stipulations described below.

Game #1

The stipulation to getting as many balls between the two pieces of string begins with an additional rule that you must not only get a chip between the strings but also short of the previous chip. See how many balls you can successfully hit abiding by those rules.

Variations:
Once you master working your way from long to short, you can progress from short to long still keeping each chip shot between the two pieces of string.

To advance your skills, you should switch clubs, change the location in which you chip from, pick a place on the green with some slope to it, or reduce the distance the strings are placed apart.

Game #2

Take on a friend with this version. Player A goes first and gets four balls within the tees which also abided by the progressively 'shorter than the previous ball' rule. Player A, on his fifth attempt, can choose to go ahead with his fifth attempt or pass. By passing, he is challenging Player B to try to beat his four balls. If Player A goes ahead with his fifth ball and successfully pulls it off, he can choose to go again or pass. Had Player A chosen to go ahead with his fifth shot and unsuccessfully completed it then Player B gets 1 point by default and starts a new game by going first. If Player A passed after completing four successful chips, Player B must try to beat that. A tie results in no points and a win results in 2 points.

CHIPPING GAMES 113

5-4-3-2-1

When playing in an actual round of golf, the closer the ball is chipped to the hole the more likely one is to make the putt for a successful up-and-down. 5-4-3-2-1 and its scoring system promote just that. Setup pennies as you see in the photo with the 1-point penny one foot away from the hole and the others one foot from each other.

The goal is to receive as few points as possible by chipping the ball in or close to the hole. Chipping the ball in the hole will give you −5 points, inside one foot is worth 1 point, inside two feet gives you 2 points, inside three feet equates to 3 points and so on. If your ball comes to rest outside of the pennies, or five-foot range, then you add 10 points to your score. This wide range of scoring makes a game against an opponent quite exciting.

Game

After setting up the pennies, you should determine nine different locations around the practice green. Hit five balls from each area hopefully accumulating very few points as you go. Add them as you proceed from location to location until you finish all nine "tee boxes." Then compare your score to that of a friend's or try to set your own personal record. If you're a golf coach, this is a great game to present to the team. Each team member can start at a different location, like a shotgun start, and work their way around the green until everyone has completed all nine locations.

CHIPPING GAMES

Around the Horn

A BASKETBALL PLAYER WORKS AROUND the hoop practicing shots from different distances and angles, having come off a pick or shooting a jump shot. This golf version is similar. Chip over a knoll, chip from uneven lies, hit from a position that will provide different breaks once the ball lands on the green, hit from a tight lie or deep rough. Place yourself and your golf ball in every sort of position that your practice green will allow. Place one foot in the bunker, restrict your backswing as if a tree were inhibiting your swing. Any shot that you've seen or encountered first hand on the course should be practiced.

Game #1

From as many locations as you'd like, place one ball at each of those areas. Choose one hole in which you will be hitting all of the golf balls toward. Once you've hit every ball, leave them on the green and place the same amount of golf balls around the green once again. This time choose a different hole and chip all of the balls toward it. Continue this process until you've chipped to all of the holes. Afterward, it will be evident which shots you did better at and which ones need more attention. Be concise and aware of every result. For instance, you may be great at a downhill chip when the hole is further away, but not so spectacular at the same downhill chip when the hole is cut close to you. You need to remember this so that you can later address any mechanical improvements that will help you with that exact shot.

Game #2

Place three balls in a row coming out from the green at two paces, four paces, and six paces. This is what is known as an 'arm.' Continue to do this at a total of four different locations. Placing the balls in different distances from the green will make you either change clubs or change your setup and technique to adapt to the change in ratio of rough to green or carry to roll. Choose only one hole on the green to hit each ball to. You're done with that arm when every ball gets within the length of the club that you used to chip with. With twelve golf balls count the number of attempts it took you to get them all within that club's length.

Fill It Up

Fill it up was a game that a wonderful young amateur golfer and student of mine and I developed one day during a lesson. We still use this game quite often in our lessons and within her practice plan.

We use a practice tube of balls like you see in the photo but you can use a shag bag full, or bag from the range.

Game

The practice tube carries twenty balls but you can use as many as you'd like. Using one hole for the entire game, hit five balls from the same place just off the green. If a ball gets within the length of that tube, you get to kick it in the hole. If you don't have a practice tube, use the length of your shag bag or a club as your measuring tool. Any chip shot that fails to get within that distance will be put back into the tube to be re-hit from a different location. After the first set of five have been hit and evaluated, toss five balls down at a different place and in a different situation just off of the green and follow the same rules. This chipping game is over when you get all of the balls inside the length of your measuring device. Challenge a friend to see who finishes the practice bag first or in the fewest number of chips.

CHIPPING GAMES 119

Every Club

Lots of golfers get used to one club when chipping. While there may be absolutely nothing wrong with that method, learning to use a variety of clubs might lead you to a more effective option when you find yourself in a tight spot. By using every club in your bag, you will be developing an extreme sense for the loft of each club as well as the trajectory and therefore, the roll that each produce. Both games below are fabulous for developing feel.

Game #1

Hit one ball with every club to the same hole. You can make a game out of it by putting out and adding up your grand total. Be sure you've used every club in your bag including your driver and putter. Proceed by finding a different place just off of the green, choosing a new hole and using every club in your bad again.

Game #2

Scenario two involves hitting one ball to every hole on the chipping green with one club. Proceed by putting the balls out. After putting them out, continue from the same location with a different club and hitting one ball to every hole on the green once again. By doing so, you'll come to realize which club may be more suitable for you in a particular situation. Keep going until you've used every club in your bag.

Even Par

The best players in the world constantly express the importance of the short game. After the completion of a televised tournament, listen to how many victors say, *I didn't hit the ball all that well today, but I still managed to win.* It's common to see the winner miss fairway after fairway but still go home with the check. While their ability to recover and hit specialty shots is due much of the credit, it wouldn't all come together without their ability to get up-and-down.

Even Par is a great game to test your chipping and putting ability. Striving to get multiple balls up-and-down, as described in the two games below, actually makes the game more challenging than what you'll experience on the course. Therefore, when you face an up-and-down situation on the golf course, knowing that you only have to get up-and-down once with one ball will be easier.

Game #1

Hit five balls to the first of seven holes then putt them in. Your even par score would be a two with each ball. So after one hole, a score of even par would be ten. Continue along to hole #2 and add your score as you go along playing all seven holes. Playing seven holes means the even par grand total would be seventy. Seventy is close to the par for most 18-hole regulation length golf courses. This game and your score clearly singles out the state of your short game and how well it compares to par. You can play this game with a group and see who wins at the completion of the seven holes or practice by yourself, like Ben Hogan.

Game #2

With this version of Even Par, you can use any number of balls and set up a course with any number of holes. For our example, we will use three balls so the hole doesn't get crowded with chip shots and play a five hole course. Hit all three balls to hole #1 and putt them in. Your even par score will be two with each ball (one chip and one putt) for an even par score of six for each hole. Set this even par number of six as your goal. This means you cannot move onto the next hole until you've reached this number. If the hole you're chipping to is quite far away or if your ability is not up to par, feel free to alter the goal number so that it is more attainable.

Under Par

CHIPPING ONE IN CAN BE the most memorable shots of your round and holing one during competition can be a shot that turns the table on your opponents. A chip-in may kick start your game as you come down the final stretch. Just ask Tiger Woods about his unbelievable chip-in at the 2005 Masters on hole number sixteen or Tom Watson at the seventeenth at Pebble Beach in 1982 when he went on to beat Jack Nicklaus.

Knocking one in the cup can refocus your energy and thrust your game to a level that shakes the play of your opponents. While this game's rules require that you chip one in, they also call for successful up-and-downs with all of your other chips.

Game

Start with five golf balls and pick a hole to chip to that is of the average length that you tend to face on the course. With an even par score of ten (one chip and one putt with each ball) you must start over if you don't score a nine or less. Putting out is mandatory even if you don't chip one in. Putting out develops discipline and perseverance even though there would be no way to score under par.

Once you've scored under par with those five balls, you've now progressed to the 10 Ball tier. At this tier an under par score of nineteen or less must be achieved in order to move on to the next tier. I suggest chipping only five balls at a time no matter what tier you're on otherwise the hole becomes too crowded and doesn't allow for a chip-in. This is a long term game that you can continue to use throughout the years. Use the scorecard at the right to help your progress and chart your successes.

SCORECARD

Number	_Score_	_Date_
5 BALLS	_____	_____
10 BALLS	_____	_____
15 BALLS	_____	_____
20 BALLS	_____	_____
25 BALLS	_____	_____
30 BALLS	_____	_____
35 BALLS	_____	_____
40 BALLS	_____	_____
45 BALLS	_____	_____
50 BALLS	_____	_____

Up-And-Down

Getting up-and-down around the green is what many rounds come down to especially when a golfer's full swing seems to have vanished and Greens In Regulation becomes a diminishing number. So much is made of the long game these days and rightfully so. It's amazing to see how far some players can hit it but the short game still needs to be a staple in your game. It needs to be one of your strengths.

Have a short game that others look up to. Be the up-and-down master. If your chip fails to drop, get excited to show off your putting skills. Never being counted out can be an intimidating trait to other competitors but it mainly comes down to how much desire you have. You must believe that you can get up-and-down from anywhere. Successful up-and-downs can be just the fist pumping momentum you need to carry on through the round.

Game #1

Pick a hole on the practice green, toss a ball somewhere within five yards of the green, followed by the club you prefer to use given the amount of green you have to work with and the amount of airtime that is required to carry the ball to your chosen landing spot. Hit the chip and if it doesn't drop, grab your putter and go knock it in. Play 9-holes adding your score as you go along. Total your score at the end of this 9-hole course. Try it again with the intention of bettering your score or record it in a game improvement journal so you can beat it the next time you practice. You can also play this same game against a friend designating the number of holes to be played. Lowest score wins.

Game #2

Pretend that you're playing eighteen holes of golf and that you've missed every green in regulation. Here are eighteen opportunities to see what you would shoot if you miss every green. With only one ball, chip the ball to a hole and proceed by putting it until it is holed. Continue this game for a total of eighteen holes. Count your score as you go along. Develop a goal and try to reach it. Much like missing green after green on the golf course wears you out and challenges your short game, this game will do the same. Which is why when you do miss some greens during the course of a round, you'll be better prepared physically and definitely mentally.

Two Ball Game

Taking a mulligan, breakfast ball or redo shouldn't be a part of anyone's game. Over time, these types of "freebies" weaken your ability to recover mentally and physically from whatever circumstance the game throws your way. Bad shots are a part of the game and what you do after hitting one will dictate your success as a golfer. In my time as an assistant college golf coach, I would often watch prospects play in tournaments waiting to see how they reacted after hitting a poor shot. You must own up to your miss-hits and misfortune and get on with it - that's what it's all about.

Against my two ball oath, this game requires that you hit two shots. The challenging twist of this game, and why I really like it, is that you must choose the worst of the two shots instead of the better one.

Game #1

Drop two balls just off the green. Proceed to chip both balls one at a time to one of the holes on the chipping green. As an example, let's say your first chip hangs on the lip and your second chip ends up five feet away. You will pick up your better ball and place it next to the five-footer. Now roll two putts from there. If one goes in and the other goes two feet past the hole, you must again pick up the better ball, which in this case is in the hole, and place it next to the two-footer. Proceed until you roll in both balls from the same spot. In our example, assuming you holed both putts from two feet, your score would be a three. Here's how: your first chip ended five feet away. Second was your putt from there that rolled two feet past the hole and the third was holing both balls from that position.

CHIPPING GAMES 129

Two Ball Game (continued)

Game #2

Play nine holes of this Two Ball Game using different clubs, hitting from different slopes, from different types of lies and to a green that varies in slope and speed. For example, hole one is a chip in which you must use your sand wedge. Hole number two is from a downhill lie. Hole number three must be hit from deep grass and so on. You can set up a scorecard that describes each hole as shown in the example below.

Scorecard

HOLE	NAME	TWO BALL SCORE
1	Sand Wedge	
2	Downhill Lie	
3	Deep Rough	
4	7-Iron	
5	Against Collar	
6	Hole Cut Close	
7	Open Face Chip	
8	Uphill Lie	
9	9-Iron	

GAME #3

Drop two balls in the grass on "tee #1" and hit both chips to that hole. Putt out if you'd like but before doing so measure the distance from the hole of the furthest ball only. Your measurement can be precise or a hypothesis. Continue playing the rest of the holes measuring the worst chip shot of each hole. Not that you want to dwell on your bad shots but by measuring your worst ball, you'll always strive to get every ball close. The better your misses are the better player you become. At the end, your total distance is something to compare against a friend or to the last time you played this game. The results will also plainly show which types of chips you need to work on in practice or with your teaching professional.

SCORECARD

HOLE	NAME	WORST BALL DISTANCE
1	Sand Wedge	
2	Downhill Lie	
3	Deep Rough	
4	7-Iron	
5	Against Collar	
6	Hole Cut Close	
7	Open Face Chip	
8	Uphill Lie	
9	9-Iron	

Sevens

SEVENS IS A GAME THAT YOU may have discovered in the putting section of this book. Its versatility allows it to be blended into a chipping version.

The established point system rewards you for chipping one in or for getting it close and punishes your score for not getting up-and-down. The scoring system is similar to what happens on your scorecard when you do the same in a round of golf. Play with a friend, your regular foursome, or your golf team to see who becomes the Sevens Champ.

Game

One person picks the first hole and hits his or her chip shot. The next person plays from the same location to the same hole followed by the remaining players. No one can putt out until all players have hit their chip shots. You may need to mark your ball as to not interfere with an opponent's chip. The first one to reach seven points is the winner and you accumulate points in the following manner:

- *If you hole your chip shot, you receive two points and everyone else receives zero.*
- *If no one holes their chip, then the person whose ball rests closest to the hole receives one point and everyone else gets zero.*
- *Everyone always must putt out. If you make your putt, successfully getting up-and-down, you receive zero points. If you miss your putt, your total shots taken would be three or more and you subtract one point from your score.*

Scoring Recap:
- Holed chip = 2 points
- Closest ball if no one holes a chip = 1 point

Then proceed by putting:
- Successful up-and-down = zero points
- Unsuccessful up-and-down = -1 point

Can't Leave Until...

You've probably incorporated this saying in some of the games you've already played. You can play any of the chipping games and use this title as your reason to reach the goal you have set.

Can't Leave Until puts pressure on you. I can't tell you how often the following situation occurs. During the course of a lesson, for example, the golfer who is working on mechanics says, "Ok, I'm going to hit one more good one then head back to the office." This often takes a while because the student just put herself in a pressure situation and has trouble working through that. But this is what golfers feel on the course. When working on mechanics it is often wise to grade yourself on the feel of your new setup or motion, not the result. At another time in your practice you should drop the mechanical thoughts and play a competitive game when the result does matter.

Below are a few examples of how to blend this game with some of the games in this section.

Game

If you're playing the 9-hole chipping game of Up-and-Down, you can't leave until you reach your stated goal of getting up-and-down six out of nine times.

When playing the Two Ball game in which you must always hit two balls and pick the worst result, you can't leave that particular hole until you've scored a two. Set that number based on your past experience and ability.

Because you should be journaling the score you make on these games you can use this game to say that you can't leave until you break the record for the particular game that you're playing.

chapter 9

PITCHING GAMES

Practicing out of divots, off hilly or perched lies, off leaves and pine needles, under and over trees, off moist and dry turf, and all other goofy situations you invariably encounter in golf, prepares you for both the expected and the unexpected.

-- Seve Ballesteros

The Bucket

The bucket can be a great game if you feel you're getting too technical. It allows you to focus on the target and the challenge of hitting a shot with the perfect trajectory, distance and direction. It will reenergize your competitive spirit and is a wonderful game for instructors to introduce to junior golfers. You can also use a trash barrel or car washing bucket from your garage.

After setting up a bucket you can either step off the distance if you're the more calculating type or not if you're the more feel type. Proceed by trying to fly a ball into it. This is something you can do if you have adequate space in your yard, at a park or in some open area at a practice facility.

Game #1

With a friend alternate hitting pitch shots and see who pitches a ball into the bucket first. You can change up the distances placing the bucket close and then farther away. Receiving one point for each ball that goes in, see who reaches ten points first. Remember that you still must alternate hitting shots. Stay away from rapid fire as it quickly takes you out of a sound routine and technique.

Game #2

Set the bucket ten yards away from you. Hit ten balls and count how many you proceed to make. Then move back to twenty yards hitting ten balls again. Jot down the number of pitches that make it in the bucket from each distance and continue outward as far back as you wish.

You will likely see that although you may not make a large percentage of the attempts, many of the balls come close which on the golf course will equate to a higher probability of making the putt.

Change It Up

On the course golfers are rarely faced with the same shot twice, and hopefully never. Practicing in the same manner is a must. The golfer who can hit pitch shot after pitch shot of the same distance and trajectory does not mean that he can change his trajectory and distance for the varying shots he'll encounter on the course. This only means that the person is good at that distance when having a multitude of balls in practice. He will still have to prove that he can do it with one ball in competition. Realistic practice is a better gauge of that probability. Pitching balls of different distances with each swing with as much precision as hitting forty in a row to one location is much more productive for playing purposes.

Game #1

After placing five towels in an open area at 10, 20, 30, 40 and 50 yards, use one ball to hit to the 30-yard towel, for instance. Then hit one ball to the 10-yard towel, then the 40-yarder, the 20-yarder and finally the 50-yard towel. The purpose is to mix it up. The scoring system for this game goes like this. If the ball hits the intended towel, you receive five points. Once you hit the first five balls to these different towels continue with four more rounds of five balls. You will have hit twenty-five balls in total. Add your score, journal it next to the day's date and beat it next time pitching is on your practice agenda.

Game #2

Against a friend and with the point system described below see which one of you can accumulate 100 points first. Start at the 10-yard towel progressing in 10-yard increments. Feel free to add towels at other distances if you wish.

One person goes first to the 10-yard towel. If this person hits the towel, five points is awarded. Then the second person goes to the same towel. If this person hits the towel, then ten points is awarded for topping the opponent. If the first person misses, zero points are awarded and only five points is given to the second player if he successfully hits the towel.

Zero points if not. The first player continues to go first through all of the towels, before switching on the next round when the second player goes first. I would advocate moving forward or back five yards after several sessions so as to work on those in between yardages.

Closest To

Closest to is just what it sounds like. The person who pitches it the closest to the hole wins. Hitting shots from different lies to different pins should also be a part of this game. Verbally prodding your buddy with a bit of chatter will add another dynamic to the game. A friend looking closely over your shoulder will test your nerves, your discipline to focus and your ability to accept outside distractions.

Game

Play with as many people as you'd like. Everyone will hit from the same location to the same pin. The person whose ball is closest gets one point while the others receive zero points. Any pitch shot that is holed is worth five points while the others are left with no points. If multiple people hole a shot on the same hole, each receives five points.

Pick a number in which all players will attempt to accumulate a point total. The winner is the one whose total points reach that number first. The person who gets closest on the previous hole gets the honor of choosing the next pin and location from which to pitch. If you get the honor, be creative with the lie and type of shot it dictates.

9-Point

While many of the games in this book can be played solo or with a countless number of people, this game does require a total of exactly three people.

Game

All three players pitch a ball to the same pin. The person whose ball is closest receives five points, the second closest receives three points, while the last person receives one point. The distribution of points will always total nine. Here are some other possible scenarios:

- *Two tie for closest: 4 points each while the third place person receives 1 point*
- *One person gets closest while two people tie for second closest: 5 points for the closest while the two people receive 2 points each.*
- *A tie among all three players means each player receives 3 points.*

In every scenario the points total nine. You can play 9-holes of pitching to see who has the highest point total at the end or set a point total to be reached and the game is over once one person hits that number. Some players agree before beginning that a pitch which comes to rest within one club length of an opponent's pitch shot is considered a tie. Set your own rules but a measuring device may be needed to settle any disputes. Using the same point system and putting out can add an added benefit and certainly clear up any disputes. If you decide to putt out, points are not awarded for whose ball was pitched closest but instead on the total number of strokes taken by each player.

Ship, Captain & Crew

Ship, captain and crew is actually a dice game that has been adopted as the official evening entertainment with one of our corporate golf clients. It has been modified to make a great pressure-packed pitching game. And while rolling the dice is based on luck, this pitching game requires more skill.

Game

An unlimited number of people can play. This golf version of Ship, Captain, and Crew requires that each person throw a quarter into the pot. The person who pitches their golf ball closer to the hole than the rest of the field gets the pot. A tie is considered a ball that lies within one foot of the closest ball. In the case of a tie, no one claims the pot and everyone throws in another quarter. The pot is essentially doubled and the order in which everyone pitches remains the same.

When there is a declared winner, that person starts first. Changing locations and pins and dropping the ball from shoulder height to see what kind of lie you get are all variations to be thrown in the mix.

Playing this game by trying to pitch it into a bucket can be useful and fun as well. It can easily be played in the backyard. Ties are given if no one makes it in the bucket or if more than one person pitches it in.

Objects

It's all too often that golfers don't properly warm up. An inadequate warm up can lead to poor ball striking, misdirected shots and very possibly an injury. Stretching should definitely be the first task you do followed by a lot of short swings with one of your wedges. For some reason many people think that just because they bought a bucket of balls they have to hit every one of them a mile to get their money's worth. On the contrary, the pitch is somewhat of a mini version of your full swing and can dramatically boost the productivity of your full swing practice.

Game

A short pitch shot can seem boring when on the driving range with the first green often 100 yards or more away but pitching the ball to other objects can be quite entertaining. Simply pitch the ball to another ball that is on the range in front of you. Pick a leaf, a discolored spot of grass or sprinkler head. Move from object to object hitting shots that vary in yardage from five to fifty. While it seems simple, this game will really capture your attention. You'll want to do it every time you practice because it's not only beneficial but attainable. It's fun to see your ball land precisely next to the small target you were aiming at. A friend or teammate next to you will likely join in and soon a contest erupts.

On the Mark

BRING ALONG A FRIEND as well as a scorecard, piece of notebook paper, or better yet, string to create a four-foot area that makes up your landing spot. In the photo, you'll see that the circular Lag Golf System is being used. Though the direction of the shot can be incorporated into this game, its purpose is to increase your feel for the distance the shot should travel.

Game

With a friend looking on, hit a pitch with your goal being to hit the landing area on a fly. The major rule to this game is that you cannot watch the ball in flight or land until you present a verbal guess to your friend based on your feel. Did the ball land too short, too long or inside the circle? If you use a scorecard or piece of notebook paper, you and your friend should decide what area around the paper makes up an acceptable distance. With regard to your eyes being closed, I would suggest that you hit the shot with your eyes open and close them as the ball leaves the clubface. After you state your guess and open your eyes, have your friend point to the exact position in which your ball landed, even if your guess was correct. You need that feedback so that you can either alter your next shot or duplicate the feel of a successful pitch. Continue this game for ten golf balls before switching roles with your friend. As you continue you should realize an increased awareness of your feel for the contact as well as the length and pace of the swing

Helpful aids may be visualizing the shot or taking practice swings rehearsing exactly the length and pace of the swing that you'll need to hit that particular shot. While this game helps increase your feel awareness, your brain and body desperately need to know where the ending goal is located. That would be the hole. It's not just about hitting your landing spot. After all, two shots of varying trajectory can land on the mark but roll out completely different distances. Therefore, make sure you have a hole that the ball is traveling toward while playing this game and place the circle in accordance with that hole.

PITCHING GAMES 147

In-Between

Position two head covers thirty feet apart on the practice green or in some area of open grass. Try to get as many pitches to come to rest between the head covers keeping in mind the rules set below.

Game #1

The stipulation to getting as many balls between the two head covers begins with an additional rule that each pitch must stop short of the previous pitch. See how many balls you can successfully hit abiding by that rule. Once you master working your way from long to short, you can progress from short to long again while staying between the two head covers. Add another dimension by switching clubs, changing the location in which you pitch from or reducing the distance between the head covers.

Game #2

Take on a friend and play this version. Player A goes first and, for instance, gets five balls within the head covers which also abided by the progressively 'shorter than the previous ball' rule. Player A, on his sixth attempt, can choose to go ahead with his sixth attempt or pass. By passing, he is challenging Player B to try to beat his five balls. If Player A goes ahead with his sixth ball and successfully pulls it off, he can choose to go again or pass. Had Player A chosen to go ahead with his sixth shot and unsuccessfully completed it then Player B gets 1 point by default and Player B starts with another game. If Player A passed after completing five successful chips, Player B must try to beat that. A tie results in no points and a win results in 2 points.

Eighteen

You may have heard some professional golfers, including Annika Sorenstam, talk about a perfect score during the course of eighteen holes being a birdie on each hole for a total of fifty-four. This pitching game includes hitting eighteen pitch shots so a perfect score of eighteen is the goal and hence the title.

This game's goal is to get each ball within a designated distance from every hole resulting in one point for every successful shot.

Pick a green that has three distinctly different hole locations. It can be three simple pins like in the photo or you can position yourself in a more challenging position by placing a bunker between you and the holes.

Game

Before pitching a ball to hole #1, hole #2 and to hole #3, predetermine a distance away from the hole that you believe each ball should come to rest. Make sure the distance you set challenges your current ability level. Once you've hit a ball to each of these holes, tally your points by receiving one point for every shot that ends up within your acceptable distance. Then start over again by pitching to the same three holes - feel free to pitch from different locations around the green. Regardless, you will pitch to these three holes a total of six times each which means you'll have hit eighteen pitch shots.

A couple of scoring variations to this game include totaling your score as described above in an effort to beat your personal record or until you've scored a perfect eighteen. You can continue to hone your pitching skills by moving further away, minimizing the distance around the hole that is acceptable or by finding three other holes that are more difficult to pitch toward. You can also take on a friend to see who scores the highest.

PITCHING GAMES 151

Fringe Benefits

Course strategy isn't often practiced around the short game area but it is an invaluable component to realistic practice. This game requires some thought and planning as well as the physical skill to pull off the shot and the mental skill to commit to it.

Game

Against one or more friends the person's pitch shot that comes to rest as close to the fringe as possible is the winner. A more realistic and challenging version is to find a situation in which you pitch to a hole with a green that slightly slopes uphill. This is the perfect opportunity to leave your ball below the hole for an easy uphill putt. So the person who pitches his or her ball as close to the hole without going past it is the winner. The opposite setup is also possible where you find a green that slopes away from you. In this case, you will strive to get your pitch to come to rest as close to the hole as possible without being short of it, again giving you an easy uphill putt for a successful up-and-down. Feel free to putt them out or just see who has accumulated the most wins after having pitched the ball a certain number of times. This scenario obviously assumes that a person prefers uphill putts over downhill putts. Other people are the opposite and prefer downhillers. If you're one of them, simply change the rules accordingly.

PITCHING GAMES 153

Leap Frog

Leap frog is a game that really enhances the precision of one's attention to the distance and direction of each pitch shot.

You just need an open area to start. Even the driving range works great. The landing area in front of you needs to be visible and the grass needs to be trimmed short enough so that each ball residing in the grass remains in sight. A ball that settles down in grass that is too long will be challenging to use.

Game

Start by hitting your first pitch shot to a distance of about five yards. That distance is not important just keep it within about ten yards of you. What is more important is your accuracy on the following pitch shots as that first ball becomes your target for the next shot. You will strive to land it on top of your first ball. It's a very small target so pat yourself on the back if you hit it. If not, it should have enough speed to go past the first ball. Proceed by hitting your next pitch again with the intent of having it land on the ball that you previously pitched. You will see that you've created a progression in distance. This is important because of the constant change to each shot you hit on the course. Also take note of your accuracy. While it's difficult to land a pitch exactly on top of another ball, you probably won't be missing by much and that equates to precision in both the direction and distance categories. It also makes your putts shorter in length; therefore the probability of you draining the putt goes up dramatically. This will make you a solid pitcher of the golf ball and something that will save your round even during your worst day of ball striking.

PITCHING GAMES 155

In the Zone

IN THE ZONE INCORPORATES game strategy into your practice. It will make you think more effectively when you have to choose and focus on an appropriate place to leave your ball.

You must choose a green that has a bunker or other hazard in front of it and at the same time, try to utilize one of the flags that is cut close to you. If a green with a hazard is not available, simply make up a hazard by lying down a few towels or outlining a hazard with several clubs.

You're striving to get your ball to end up in an acceptable area. To define this area, I suggest you use two lengths of string. One dictates the border closest to you and the other defines the border furthest away.

Game

With a hole that is cut this close to the edge of the green, the perfect shot would just barely carry the bunker, land in the rough, bounce a couple of times, then roll the few feet there is between the fringe and hole before dropping in the cup. The problem with this is that a shot which hits inches short of the "perfect" landing spot can end up rolling back into the bunker. All golfers have some range of error to their shots. A beginner golfer may have a wide margin of error and a professional somewhat small. The point is that we're all human and we're going to mess up at times. That said, you need to pick a landing spot which if you hit the ball a little short or long, the ball will still end up in a satisfactory position defined by the strings.

Keeping the ball out of the hazard is a must. Sometimes, in difficult situations, a ball that ends up in the rough is deemed acceptable however a ball that is on the green is typically easier to hole than one you have to chip. Get the ball on the green even if it goes twenty feet past the hole.

Hit ten shots from the same place accumulating points. You receive two points if it ends up in the designated zone. Zero points are awarded if your ball comes to rest outside of the zone, either short or long, as long as it doesn't roll into the hazard. Deduct three points for any shot that ends up in the hazard. Play against a friend or tally your own points for your personal record.

Call the Shot

This is a creative game both in the ability to dream up different shots and also to have the skill to pull them off. Both the range and short game area are adequate places to play this game and test your ability against a friend.

After the game has been completed, try to remember the shots that you didn't have much success with and ask yourself if it was due to the pressure of the situation or the physical inability to hit the shot. If the answer was the pressure, then play competitive games like this one as often as possible to become more comfortable with pressure. If it was the latter, then physically practice those shots afterward by yourself or with your teacher.

Game #1

You will call the shot that you intend to hit before hitting it. You can call such things as which pin, the shot's height and the landing spot. You can add that it will spin a lot or that it will release to the hole. Use the terrain around you to create a realistic shot. After calling the shot then proceed by hitting it. After the first player's shot, the second player will then attempt to duplicate the shot. See who pulls off the shot with more accuracy. Alternate calling the shot and play using a point system. Hit twenty shots, perhaps with the winner of each shot receiving one point. The victor is the one with the most points after those twenty shots have been hit.

Game #2

Setup over the ball with your normal grip, stance, and ball position. Have some fun by purposefully messing around with a friend. During your backswing, your buddy will call the shot for you. On the downswing you will have to adapt in order to pull off the called shot. This greatly enhances your adaptability and feel for the shot and club. While it seems challenging, you'll do quite well with a few shots under your belt.

Your friend can call the landing spot, the hole, the trajectory, or other target that is available. But keep the guidelines to one or two variables. For instance, you can say "high fringe" which means a shot that travels high and lands on the fringe. Don't make it overly demanding by stating more than two guidelines. You can get your friend back by switching roles.

End Zone

WHILE A GREEN AND FLAGS ARE NOT necessary it does give the appearance more similar to the course. Where I teach, there is a wonderful small green developed specially for pitching and the flags that are present work great with this game. We just add a practice basket in the middle or a towel as you can see in the photo. You can set up a similar area in your yard with a bucket or towel in the middle and a headcover on each side.

Game

Position the head covers ten yards apart with a towel spread out on the ground in the middle of them. You can also set up borders short and long of the towel also ten yards apart. This boundary is considered the End Zone. The point system encourages accuracy while it discourages missed shots. Five points is awarded for a shot that hits the towel or bucket. Two points for a shot that ends up in the end zone and one point must be subtracted for any shot that comes to rest outside of the end zone.

Hit ten balls seeing how high you can score or compete against a friend. If you play against a friend or your teammates, remember to alternate shots and go through your routine as you would in competition. Frequently altering the yardage of the pitch shots will make it more realistic.

- *5 points for hitting the towel/basket*
- *2 points for a ball that missed the towel/basket yet stops within the end zone*
- *-1 point for a ball that ends up outside the zone*

Half Shot

Quite frequently, you'll come across a wide array of distances from which to pitch. Even if you're trying to lay up to a specific distance, say fifty yards, your lay up shot may take an awkward bounce. For example, a ball can unexpectedly kick forward several yards. On another hole, an expected forward kick might be met with a ball that lands on a soft spot. A lay up shot can also be struck poorly resulting in an unplanned and awkward distance to the hole. All will likely leave you with odd distances and your success will depend on your level of adaptability and versatility. Preparation for the unexpected is crucial both mentally and physically. If you successfully practice the broad range of possible distances, you're less likely to be mentally shaken when it happens. Whether you like to calculate the distance or simply see how far away the target is this game can be beneficial for both methods.

Game

The goal is to hit each ball half the distance of the previous ball. Pitch the first ball a certain distance. For sake of explanation, we'll say it went seventy-five yards. Your next shot should come to rest half of that distance or approximately thirty-eight yards. Your third shot will then come to rest half of that distance or nineteen yards, your fourth shot approximately ten yards and so on. Keep going until your current shot needs to only travel a couple of yards. Once completed, start over by pitching your first shot a completely different distance. This will create an entirely different set of yardages for the remainder of your pitch shots. This is a great game that will cover a wide array of distances whether calculated or felt.

Horse

THE GOAL WITH HORSE IS TO BE ABLE to successfully pull off a shot better than your opponent. The veteran Horse player will know his opponent's weaknesses and try to develop a strategy around them.

One of the fun aspects of this game is that you can change the word you choose to spell. Instead of spelling "horse," you can spell three letter words if your time is short or long words if you're enjoying the company.

Game

Player A goes first. If Player A pulls off the pitch shot and Player B fails to do so, Player B accumulates a letter which in the case of HORSE is the letter "H." If Player B pulls off the shot, then Player A chooses another shot and goes first again. If Player A is unsuccessful in his attempt, Player B now gets to choose the shot and the roles become reversed. The first one to spell the word *horse* loses.

An important rule that needs to be set before starting should be to define exactly what a "successful" and "unsuccessful" shot is. One example of how to determine this could be that the ball must come to rest within one club length of the hole. Two or three club lengths may be more realistic but the person initiating the shot can set the distance he or she wishes and that distance can be changed for every pitch shot hit. You can use a driver to measure with or a flagstick. A group of two to four people is a comfortable number to participate in this game at one time.

5-4-3-2-1

Setup pennies on the green coming out from the hole in four different directions. Each row will include five pennies. The pennies closest to the hole, designated as the 1-point pennies, will be one yard away from the hole and the others one yard further out. This means that the 5-point pennies are five yards or fifteen feet away from the hole. The closer the ball is pitched to the hole the more likely one is to make the putt for a successful up-and-down. 5-4-3-2-1 promotes just that.

Game

The goal is to receive as few points as possible by pitching the ball close or better yet, in the cup. Pitching it in the hole will give you a –5 points, inside one yard is worth 1 point, inside two yards gives you 2 points and so on. If your ball comes to rest outside of the last penny or five-yard range then you add 10 points to your score. This wide range of scoring will allow a competition against a friend to always be a close match.

After setting up the pennies, you should determine nine different locations around the practice green. I would highly advocate hitting one ball from each tee area but multiple balls will suffice as long as you're combining it with a contest against yourself or friend. Add your points as you proceed from tee to tee until you finish all nine locations where you compare your score to a friend's or try to set your own personal record. This is a great game for a golf team to play during practice. A season long tournament among the team can set the stage for competitive, productive and realistic practices.

PITCHING GAMES

Sevens

If you've played some games from the Putting or Chipping sections within this book, you've likely come across Sevens and already know how it works. If not, just grab a buddy, your short clubs and a putter and head to the practice green.

Game

Choose some shots around the green that you encounter on the course. Over a bunker, over a mound or from an uneven lie are just a few. The consistent theme in this book is to create realistic situations and add pressure. Getting used to these situations and welcoming them, without fear, will help your confidence and focus so that come the time you're faced with a pressure situation on the course you know you'll pull it off. This scoring system helps recreate the atmosphere of the course.

Here's how it works:
- *2 points for a pitch that is holed*
- *If no one holes their pitch, then the person whose ball is closest receives 1 point*

Everyone must then putt out.
- *If your stroke total equates to two, you receive zero points*
- *If it equates to three or more you need to subtract a point from your score*

The person whose ball was closest gets to choose the next hole and location in which to pitch. The first person to seven points wins but feel free to lower the point goal if you're short on time. This type of scoring system really puts emphasis on the precision of your wedges and getting up-and-down. If allowed, this game will reward your persistence. For instance, if your pitch is far away from the hole, rolling one in with the putter can swing the momentum in your direction as your buddies shake their heads in disbelief. They had counted you out and began to score you with a negative point. Now you're back in the flow let alone a point closer to winning.

Can't Leave Until...

The title of this game starts a sentence that you need to complete. Below are some examples of how you can incorporate this saying into the games from this pitching section.

This game puts the pressure on you, which is what you want if you listen to the best players in the world. They welcome the pressure because feeling it tells them that they're playing well and that there is an opportunity to rise to the challenge. Practice this challenge by putting the pressure on you and see how confident you become after your next successful bout with your buddies, your next tournament or your personal record on the golf course.

With this game it is easy to hurry through the shots, so remember that it is not a race. Take the amount of time that helps you perform at your best and just as you would in a tournament. Go through your routine process both mentally and physically.

Games

The Bucket game is a simple example that you can't leave until you pitch one ball into the bucket. Maybe one isn't good enough for you and you determine that you can't leave until you make ten. If dinner, homework or the kids come calling, go back to the game at the earliest opportunity. Don't forever walk away from a self-made challenge.

Use the game In The Zone to say that you can't leave until you get eight out of ten in the zone or choose some other number scenario that is suitable for your ability.

Objects can be used in the same manner. Say something like, "I will not leave until I land a ball on the sprinkler head" or whatever object you're using as your target.

chapter 10

BUNKER GAMES

If I am one of the greats, it's for one simple reason; no bunker shot has ever scared me and none ever will ... Approach every bunker shot with the feeling you are going to hole it.

-- Gary Player

Three Lies

Approaching the bunker that just engulfed your ball can produce a feeling of anxiety as you peek over its edge to see what kind of fate you've been dealt.

The lies you can get in the bunker are often precarious and tend to vary every time your ball lands in one. Hard sand, soft sand, a buried ball, a ball that rolled back into its own landing mark and one that is sitting in someone's footprint are all possible.

Three Lies helps you vary that lie in practice so that you can be better prepared for them when you play.

Game

Place three balls in the bunker each with a different lie. The ball on the left is a good lie resting nicely on top of the sand. The ball in the middle is half-buried and the ball on the right hit the sand and rolled back into its own landing mark. Hit one ball at a time to the same flag. Your purpose can vary but one example would be to continue by putting all three of them out. You can set a stroke total as your goal. A different version would be to get each ball within a designated circumference of the hole. Continue doing so until you get all three shots within that circumference a total number of times that you choose.

Three Targets

You need a bunker and a green that has three flags on it. If your practice bunker green only has one or two holes on it, see if your superintendent will cut another hole or two into the green. Ideally, those holes will be placed in a fashion that forces your bunker shots to vary in distance. If not, seek out other golf courses in your area and hopefully you'll find one that has an adequate practice bunker facility.

This is a great game that will teach you to vary the length of your bunker shots. Golfers vary the length of their bunker shots in numerous ways. Some take a shallower or deeper divot. Some make their divot entry point closer to or further from the ball and some by altering the length and/or pace of their swing. Some simply change clubs. Others find a personal method by blending several of these effective processes together.

Game #1

Hit one shot to the nearest flag, then one to the second flag and finally to the far flag. The degree of acceptability in the result of each shot does depend on your ability. You should set one for yourself. An example would be to develop a diameter of ten feet that every shot must get within. Encircle the hole with string to show this boundary or simply use a club to measure with.

Game #2

Hit one ball to each hole and proceed to putt them out. Set a goal for yourself. Continue this exercise for a total of six times. This means that you'll have hit eighteen bunker shots. You can tally your total as you go or record your up-and-down percentage, otherwise known as a *sandy*, in your journal.

Some notable information for you is that the top players in the world get up-and-down from the sand an average of around 50%.

BUNKER GAMES 173

✓ "Knock Out" 3 x 3

THIS GAME WILL HELP YOU DEVELOP better feel for the distance that your bunker shots travel. Take note of the superb bunker play of the tour pros. They commonly get the ball close or in the hole from the bunker and many have won a tournament by holing a bunker shot on the last hole. Most would rather be in a bunker than the deep rough surrounding a green because they find they can control the flight, spin and therefore result much easier.

Game

Begin by hitting one shot to the edge of the green that is closest to you - try to barely get it on. Your next bunker shot should come to rest three yards past your first shot. Proceed by hitting each shot three yards further than the previous bunker shot. You will have to learn to control the size, depth and entry point of your divots in order to control the spin, height and distance of the ball.

At any point, you can alter this game by hitting your first shot far and working your way closer to you. In this case, you should begin by hitting your first shot toward the far end of the green. Then each shot after that should come to rest three yards short of the previous bunker shot.

You can play this game as many times as you'd like. Remember that if one of your shots doesn't quite end up three yards from the previous shot just continue from wherever that last shot ended. Don't let it inhibit your ability to get on with the show. Instead, let a poor shot be a mental trigger for you to show off your talents.

5-4-3-2-1

SETUP PENNIES AS YOU SEE in the photo with the 1-point penny one foot away from the hole and the others one foot from each other. This will mean that the 5-point penny is five feet away from the hole. Feel free to adjust the pennies to distances better suited for your ability

The goal is to receive as few points as possible by hitting each ball as close as possible. Holing a shot from the bunker is always a fun surprise and worth a subtraction of five points from your score. Hitting it inside the one-foot penny is worth one point, inside the two-foot penny gives you two points, inside the three-point penny equates to three points and so on. If your ball comes to rest outside of the last penny, then you add ten points to your score. This wide point accumulation process creates a game that always seems to come down to the last shot. Never being out of it and never assuming that you're going to win are things to live by in competitive golf.

Game

After setting up the pennies and hitting five balls to that hole, you can change holes. Place the pennies at a different hole and proceed again from the bunker. You can even change the lie of your ball with each round. Add your points as you go until you have finished hitting five shots to every hole on the green. If you only have one or two holes on your practice green you can simply start over from a different bunker or different place within the bunker.

This game may entice you to practice your bunker shots more often. Having a stellar short game doesn't just mean from the grass. You've got to be able to get up-and-down from anywhere. Compare your score to a friend's or try to set your own personal best.

BUNKER GAMES 177

Four Slopes

In a bunker it's common to find your ball on a slope. Uphill, downhill or the two side hill lies in which the ball is either above your feet or below it are the four basic ones.

These four, as well as a combination of them, is what you will experience on the course. They all need to be practiced but to start, you should practice the four common lies and grasp the adjustments that you need to make in order to be successful. You will begin to become a more skilled bunker player and better prepared for the various situations that each bunker shot presents.

Game

Choose one flag on the green. Create a predetermined distance around the hole that would be acceptable to you - perhaps that's fifteen feet. In any order, hit one ball from an uphill lie then one ball from a downhill lie. Continue by hitting a shot with the ball above your feet and another with the ball below your feet all to the same flag. After hitting all four shots, those balls that come to rest inside the boundary are worth one point. Those that are outside of that boundary have a zero point value. However, you continue by putting out. Any putt that is holed from outside of that boundary receives two points. Any putt that is made from within your boundary is worth one point. Giving yourself two points for a putt made from outside of that boundary trains you to not give up even though your bunker shot was less than desirable.

Continue this game as many times as you'd like. For instance, you can play nine rounds of Four Slopes for a total of thirty-six bunker shots and accompanying putts. Test your ability each time you play by challenging your score from a previous day of practice or take on a friend to see who scores the highest.

Ball Below Feet   Ball Above Feet

Uphill Lie   Downhill Lie

BUNKER GAMES 179

"PLAY 7" SEVEN LIES

THIS GAME IS A COMBINATION OF Four Slopes and Three Lies which are games previously described in this chapter. You will place seven balls in the bunker as described below.

The goal is to get each shot within your designated border if not in the hole. There is a scorecard attached to this game that will help you see which lies give you the most trouble. Of course, the more shots you hit, the more accurate your statistics will be. Therefore, use the scorecard each time you practice this game. When you play, however, you shouldn't dwell on what ails you but instead envision the best shot you can hit, be decisive and committed and then execute the shot.

GAME

Determine a boundary around the hole that would be an acceptable distance for where your bunker shots should come to rest. You can use string, the Lag Golf System, a tailor's tape measure or simply step it off.

Hit one ball from seven different lies. They include a good lie, a half-buried lie, a lie in which the ball rolls back into its own landing mark, ball below feet, ball above feet, an uphill lie and finally a downhill lie.

Tally each shot with a one if it comes to rest inside of your predetermined border or a zero if it does not. Hit each of these seven lies as many times as you'd like. Perhaps you hit each shot ten times. Place that number just below the date on the scorecard so you know how many out of ten you pulled off.

Scorecard

Date: _____/_____/_____
Number of shots hit: _____

LIE	**SCORE**
Good	_____
Landing Mark	_____
Half-buried	_____
Uphill	_____
Downhill	_____
Ball Above Feet	_____
Ball Below Feet	_____

Fairway Bunker 5x5

Every Green Fairway Bunker

MOST OF THE TIME GOLFERS only practice their fairway bunker shots when they encounter them during a round. While you should be learning from every shot that is hit, this really isn't practice.

If you struggle with them and don't have a place at your practice facility designated for fairway bunker shots, use the course late in the evening or very early in the morning when it's less busy. There also may be a practice facility close to you that does have a fairway bunker. It's likely to be unoccupied and ready for you.

Game

Designate an area around each target on the range as your acceptable boundary. This might be the green surrounding the flag or some area around each of your targets. In our example, there are six flags on the range. Hit ten balls to each flag and record how many out of ten stop within the boundary. This will give you a starting point. From there you will make some goals as to how many you'd like to hit. Then begin trying to accomplish it.

Let's imagine there are six flags on the range. Their yardages are laid out on the scorecard you will find on the next page. Keeping track of your development with the use of this scorecard can be quite beneficial. On the left side of the scorecard is a description of each target and the yardage. The yardages will likely stay the same from day to day as long as you don't move too far forward or back in the bunker. Write down your goal and then the number that actually stopped within your boundary followed by the date.

You can even practice different lies or circumstances. A common one is factoring in the trajectory that the ball needs to come out on in order to avoid catching the lip. Coming to a solid conclusion as to what you can realistically do with this or any sort of lie before you're faced with it on the course will save you strokes.

Scorecard

TARGET	GOAL	# HIT	DATE
Yellow Flag (77 yds)			
Black Flag (113 yds)			
Purple Flag (125 yds)			
White Flag (140 yds)			
Green Flag (152 yds)			
Red Flag (184 yds)			

BUNKER GAMES 183

Five Ball Fairway Bunker

Successfully firing one out of a fairway bunker can be a daunting task but with some practice this shot will become more attainable. After things like aim and formulating a plan for escaping the bunker, the shot comes down to decent contact and the ball avoiding the lip of the bunker on its departure. Choosing a club that has enough loft to elevate the ball over the lip is mandatory.

The bunker is a hazard and although the bunkers on the tours are well-kept, those at most clubs could use some attention. You can get terrible lies or inconsistent sand depths but it is what it is. If you're in trouble, get the ball safely back into play. The game of golf will allow you some misfires but only to a degree. A well-thought out plan, which includes your club and target choice, will make your margin of error greater and consequently your success rate.

This fairway bunker game asks you to grade the result of each shot. Thankfully, in golf as a whole, you don't have to hit perfect shots in order to shoot a great score. It may not be picture perfect but if it works then it's effective.

Game

Grab a short iron and then every other club after that perhaps even a lofted fairway wood. You will hit five balls with each club giving yourself a score for each ball hit. Give yourself one point if the result is acceptable and subtract a point if it's unacceptable. Set yourself and each ball a different distance away from the edge of the bunker. Take the lie and the lip of the bunker into consideration when judging your score.

You should always have a target and it's likely that there won't be flags that match your clubs' yardages. Find a target in the background or a discoloration of grass on the range that suits the distance of that club.

BUNKER GAMES 185

Can't Leave Until

Can't leave until can be a frustrating but growing experience. It is up to you to complete the sentence. Here are a few examples:

- *Can't leave until I hole one from the bunker.*
- *Can't leave until I get ten in a row out of the bunker and onto the green.*
- *Can't leave until I get a certain score when playing the fairway bunker games.*
- *Can't leave until I reach my set goal for the Seven Lies game.*
- *Can't leave until I get five in a row inside six feet of the hole.*

chapter 11

FULL SWING GAMES

Instead of just hitting balls, make believe every ball represents a shot during the round. Actually visualize the course conditions — where the pin is cut, where the bunkers are, how the match stands.
-- Nancy Lopez

Every Green

Find a practice facility near your home that has several targets on the range. Flagsticks on greens are the best but other target options will work fine. While the flag will not always be your target on the course, most flags on the range are positioned in the center of each green making the area of the green encompassing the flagstick fairly equal.

Feel free to use yardage signs, posts or other objects that may be positioned on your driving range. In this case you will have to set up an imaginary boundary around that target that would constitute an acceptable border for your shots.

Game

In this example, there are six flags on the range. Begin by choosing a total number of balls you intend to hit to each flag. Perhaps it is ten. If you're unsure of your ability, hit those ten balls and see how many come within your boundary. But after that, the true part of the game, the pressure and the feelings that come with it, come with setting a goal. Determine a number of shots out of ten that you want to strive toward. The flags that are closer to you, should have a higher goal as they're easier shots. You can incorporate this game into each practice session trying to better your score. A scorecard is available to track each session. On the left describes each target and the yardage. The yardages may change from day to day as the hitting area on the tee moves forward or back from the previous day. The day to day change in yardage will force you to use different clubs and hit shots between clubs. On the scorecard, state your goal and then the number that actually hit the green followed by the date. Develop your own scorecard perhaps with the yardage left blank so that you can fill that in each day and use them in other practice sessions.

SCORECARD

TARGET	GOAL	# HIT	DATE
Yellow Flag (92 yds)			
Blue Flag (116 yds)			
Red Flag (162 yds)			
White Flag (169 yds)			
Yellow Flag (196 yds)			
Black Flag (261 yds)			

9-Ball

ALL YOU NEED IS A FEW RANGE BALLS and a buddy to compete against. The game 9-Ball is taken from the billiard game by the same name. If you haven't played 9-Ball before in pool have no worries. It's easy to follow and just takes some creativity in setting up.

Game

You have to hit shots in an order predetermined before starting. An example is described below but yours will be unique to the practice facility you're on. Each player must successfully perform the shot at hand starting with shot #1 before moving on to shot #2 and so on. Player A goes first with shot #1. If the result coincides with the predetermined shot, the player proceeds to shot #2. If the player misses any of the shots, then Player B starts at shot #1. If the result is successful that same player proceeds to the next shot. If unsuccessful the other player picks up where he or she left off. The first one to complete shot #9 successfully wins.

Shot #1: Hit green with orange flag

Shot #2: Hit green with yellow flag

Shot #3: Driver between the tree and pink flag

Shot #4: Must fly into bunker

Shot #5: Hit green with purple flag

Shot #6: Fade toward tree

Shot #7: Draw to green with white flag

Shot #8: Ball lands between white and purple flags

Shot #9: Must hit tree

Be sure to differ each of the predetermined shots so that the club you're hitting changes from shot to shot. Every range has a unique look. The backdrop and targets differ from range to range which is what makes it fun to create these nine shots. The pressure and realistic approach of this game comes with only getting one attempt at a time.

Play Golf

Just as the title states, you're going to play golf on the range. In order to simulate a golf course while on the range, you should imagine your home course, your favorite course or any course you're familiar with.

If you'll be participating in a tournament soon, playing this game imagining yourself on that course will be exceptionally helpful. Seeing yourself at that tournament and feeling its surroundings can work wonders. Doing so can help your nerves, your game plan, comfort level and confidence when you do actually set foot on the course. This game is a rehearsal just as practice should be.

If hole #1 requires that you hit a 3-wood, pull it out of your bag and hit it on the range with a boundary of the fairway "imprinted" onto the range. You can use other range targets as borders to your imaginary fairway. If you've played that course before and are quite familiar with it, you should even picture each target off of the tee while hitting that ball on the range. If you strike it solidly and on line, perhaps you'll have a 6-iron in to the green. Grab your six, find a similar target as you would on the course, go through your routine, and let it go. If you hit your target as though it would have been on the putting surface go ahead and proceed onto hole #2. If a putting green is near, go ahead and putt. If your 6-iron failed to land on the green, grab one of your wedges and pitch the ball to a target close to you as though you were trying to get up-and-down during the tournament. That target can be a flag, a sprinkler head, a ball or anything that resembles the distance your 6-iron shot was from the target.

Play each hole and shot with a target in mind. Go through your routine and though you may have this perfect round of golf in your mind, the game of golf throws all sorts of things at you so at the same time you're cruising through this "practice round" also sense that you can adapt and recover from whatever situation arises. No matter what it is, you'll be able to overcome it and persevere.

If possible, find a place on the range where you can hit from the rough if need be or from a hilly lie. You can even kick a ball over from the range bucket and play the ball from wherever it comes to rest. Play all 18-holes as it won't take very much time. If you couldn't putt during this "round," I would recommend rolling a few after your range time and before you go home. During this game, feel the tournament, the surroundings and the pressure - it'll really help once you do set foot on the course.

Five Ball Game

BEING ABLE TO HIT SHORT IRONS, middle irons, long irons, and woods is a good mix but the premise to this game is your occupation in bettering your score. That is what will put the pressure on and consequently allow you to play better when the pressure rises on the course.

You will be scoring yourself on the result of each shot. You will hit poor shots in golf but if the result works out then so be it. Don't get overly consumed in the perfection of the strike. To improve as a golfer however, you will have to come to understand that the process which is adhered to before you hit the ball is most crucial. The time spent hitting the shot is just that. Get engrossed in, attached to and connected to the shot you're about to hit as well as the target.

This game came from my days working with Mike McGetrick who teaches many of the top players on the LPGA Tour.

[handwritten: Five Ball / Five Club - One Target]

Game #1

Your club choice may depend on your wedge make-up but let's start with your sand wedge. Choose a target that represents the appropriate distance. Hit five balls with your sand wedge to that target and score yourself with a +1 point for an acceptable result or a –1 point for an unacceptable result. Then move to your 9-iron and hit five more balls using the same scoring system. Using a sand wedge, 9, 7, 5, and 3 irons along with a couple of woods you will have hit thirty-five shots. Scores usually aren't high due to the subtraction of a point for an unacceptable result. For instance, if half of your results are acceptable and the other half are not, your score would be zero.

Depending on your time, you can use every club in your bag or every other. Use your even numbered clubs one day as shown in the photo and your odd numbered clubs another.

Game #2

Mixing in an imaginary golf course on the range with this Five Ball Game presents a unique game that forces you to change clubs with each shot. Play nine or eighteen holes on the range just as you would if you were on the course but use the Five Ball Game scoring system - one point for an acceptable result and a minus one point for an unacceptable result. On par 3 holes you will only hit one shot. On par 4 holes, you'll hit two shots and par 5 holes will require three shots. Count your score as you go along until you've completed your last hole. Record your score in your practice journal and strive to set a personal record next time out.

Five Ball Mental Game

THE SCORING SYSTEM IS EXACTLY like that of the Five Ball Game on the previous page but what you will be grading is different.

It is quite common that to improve your game, you must improve the way you think and act on the course. This mental version of the Five Ball Game works your heart and mind. Mentally, hitting a golf ball typically requires that one does more erasing what is in one's head than it does adding to what's in a golfer's brain. Simplify your time over the ball by being engrossed in your target and committing to it before swinging away. What precedes your shot may be more analytical that what goes on during the shot. During this game, you will be grading your routine, your preparatory skills and your full commitment to your target. Anything less than full receives a minus point.

Game

Before you even pull a club out of your bag you need to come into every shot with an open mind not having many, if any, preceding thoughts. Every shot in golf is different even the same par 3 hole at your home course may require a different shot from day to day. The location of each tee box and pin, course conditions, weather, wind, your body and other factors all paint a different picture from day to day and shot to shot.

Evaluate things like yardage, wind direction and velocity, temperature, the lie of the ball, any elevation change, the location of hazards and obstacles, your ball striking that day, humidity, any curvature your shots tend to have and the surface of the landing spot are all factors that you should take into consideration before choosing a target and then club. This can take some time which is why the time to hurry in golf is between shots. You need to do some thinking and evaluating here. The lack of attention to these will likely cause you to miss the shot before you hit it. Once you've pulled the appropriate club. You must commit to it. Continue to go through the mental and physical steps to your routine as you address the ball, align yourself appropriately, commit and swing away. You will often hear players of every sport after a remarkable performance say that they got out of their own way. That is what you're trying to create and that is what will be created once you organize yourself and your thinking. Time in golf is completely different from most sports. The most common sports are reactionary while golf is proactive therefore you need to structure your thoughts into a sound process that works for you. If you have successfully gone through this pre-swing process, committed and swung freely you deserve more that one point but that's what the rules of this game permit. Hit five balls each with as many clubs as you'd like. Each complete dedication to your routine and commitment receives a plus point. A skipped step, failed process or negative thought when hitting the ball results in a minus point.

> A high handicapper will be surprised at how often the mind will make the muscles hit the ball to the target, even with a far less than perfect swing.
>
> -- Harvey Penick

CRICKET

THE GAME CRICKET DERIVED from a dart game of the same name was introduced to me by a college golfer and student of mine. He and his teammates would use this game to compete against each other during the team's practices.

GAME

In the dart game Cricket the object is to throw your three darts at the starting number which is the number twenty. Then your opponent attempts to throw his three darts at the number twenty. You continue alternating throwing three darts at a time. Once you get three darts in the twenty, you proceed onto the number nineteen again trying to get three darts in the number nineteen followed by three darts in eighteen, seventeen, sixteen, fifteen and finally three bulls-eyes. The first one to get three bulls-eyes is the winner.

Translating this game into golf doesn't take much. You need to start by setting a course on the range. Picking all of the greens on the range is one way but use other objects on the range or in the background as targets and borders to define each shot. In this example, the greens on the range will be the targets. In a particular order you must hit the first green three times before moving on to the second green. Just like the dart game you will hit three consecutive shots before your opponent hits three shots. You do not need to hit each target three consecutive times, just three times total. The first one to hit all of the greens three times each is deemed the winner.

Who Can Hit...

(handwritten: Groups of three op 4)

WHO CAN HIT … is a game in which you fill in the blank. You complete the sentence with some sort of golf shot.

Practice ranges have different looks to them. Some have palm trees, evergreens or maple trees surrounding them. Some have yardage signs, poles, flags, colored posts or other objects standing there waiting for you to be creative.

Game

Begin the game by dreaming up a shot like, who can hit the ball the highest. You'll tend to go right to your most lofted wedge but toss in some additional guidelines. For instance, you must use your 8-iron or 5-iron or whatever club you'd like and see who can hit the highest shot with that club. See who can hit it the lowest with your sand wedge that goes at least fifty yards. See who can hit the biggest slice and then the biggest hook. Challenge each other by seeing who can spin the ball the most or who comes closest to hitting the 100 yard post. Beginning with the same number of golf balls, see who can hit the post first. The range is your blank canvas and also your classroom for your future success on the course.

> *Imagination is more important than knowledge.*
> -- Albert Einstein

The best education institutions are ones that require realistic hands-on work take place during a person's education and not just memorizing information and regurgitating it on a test. This practice game demands the same of your golf game. Purposeful practice is one that creates real experiences.

Imaginary Fairway

This is a common game taught by instructors. If you've ever participated in a golf school or have taken a full swing lesson on driving the ball you've likely heard this one.

Every swing you make should have some similar feeling or look to it as the actual shot on the course. This game creates just that.

On the range, make out a fairway either with the flags on the range, objects in the background or anything else that can represent a left and right border. Many older driving ranges, especially in the east have a couple of trees on the range. I think golfers would be better prepared mentally for the course had their practice range been designed to look more like the golf course. So while in reality this isn't the case at most ranges, it is up to you to use what is on the range to make up a fairway.

Game #1

Each day you practice your driving skills you need to measure it against how it would hold up in competition. You can do this by hitting a certain number of balls. Let's say fourteen since that's the typical number of par 4s and 5s on a course. Not that you'll always use your driver but that is a good place to begin. The course layout matched with your game and the situation will dictate whether you use your driver or not on each of those holes. You can see how many out of fourteen you get within your imaginary fairway. Know that the best drivers in the world average around 80% yet those aren't always the best players in the world because as you know, there's much more to the game than just hitting that ridiculously expensive club. Other current and very successful tour players only hit around 55-60% of the fairways. Set your own goal and strive to reach it.

An important part about driving the ball is the condition of your bad drives. If a bad drive ends up just off of the fairway and not in trouble then you should be in good shape. But a drive that travels too far off of the fairway can cause an added half shot or more to your score. I would suggest using additional objects on the range or in the background to create a secondary border. This border should simulate the width of the playable rough at your course. You can use a point system in order to develop a new game. A ball in the fairway is worth one point. A ball that resides in the secondary border has no point value and one that travels outside of it will cost you two points.

Game #2

Imaginary Fairway Game #2 is devised in a manner so that you can find out which club is the most likely to find the fairway under pressure.

Hit ten balls each with your driver, a fairway wood and your longest iron. With an imaginary fairway set up on the range, which club do you find hits the fairway more consistently? Doing this over an extended amount of time will show more of a trend. This trend will show which of those clubs is more reliable. It also may show that you have an ill-fitted club. Such an issue should be apparent to you if you have no problem getting the ball in the fairway with a couple of those clubs but struggle with one in particular.

Call the Shot

Like Babe Ruth at the plate pointing at the bleachers in the outfield before belting one over the fence, this game, while not surrounded by thousands of people, will create pressure and more importantly an intent and desire to pull it off.

While you won't be hitting home runs you will be calling the shot you intend to hit before you hit it. It can be a draw, a high shot, or a big hook. Get creative and hit shots that may be unordinary like a 4-iron that goes 125 yards, or a fairway wood that goes eight feet off the ground and only 150 yards as if you needed to punch it low under some tree limbs and back into the fairway.

Like stating your New Year's resolution to a friend, calling the shot before you hit it creates ownership. Such a declaration also creates a mindset in which this is the only shot that matters. This is the same mindset you should have on the golf course. The most important shot in golf is the one you're about to hit. Not the previous one or the next one, but this one.

Game #1

Standing on the range with at least one more person, alternate calling and hitting a particular shot. Perhaps you call a draw to the yellow flag. The person whose ball draws and ends up closest to the yellow flag wins. Feel free to set up your own point system if you'd like.

This game is also pretty simple to play by yourself. Develop your own scenario like so many junior golfers do. If you could get inside the brains of millions of youth golfers as they're practicing, you'd hear echoes of an announcer: *"We're on the 72nd hole at the Masters and Jonny's got to fade this tee shot starting it at the left bunker and letting it fall to the center of the fairway. He'll put himself in perfect shape to win his first Masters and be welcomed into the elite group of golfers who own a major championship. He's about ready to hit. Let's see how he does."* Then Jonny proceeds to hit the shot in practice. Whether Jonny ever makes it to the Masters or not, he is preparing himself for a pressure-packed shot in which the tournament's outcome falls in his hands.

GAME #2

I first played this game on the range of the golf course I grew up playing as a kid, Hyland Hills Golf Club in Westminster, Colorado. I played it with a great friend, Brian "Bubba" Carlson, who like so many other people I grew up playing with and working with there, is still in the golf business as a head professional.

After addressing the ball and during the backswing, your friend will call out the shot you are to hit. You will have to alter your motion and be creative not mechanical to pull it off. You can with great success and you'll realize that you did this not because you had to think about the components of the swing but that your natural talent, creativity and adaptation just allowed the shot to occur.

Line 'Em Up

Try to get to the range early in the morning or after it's been picked clean of other range balls. While it's not necessary to see your shots sitting on the driving range in the place in which they came to rest, the "painting" of your shots can be interesting to observe.

At our academy, we have three practice holes. Two par 3 holes and one par 4 hole. This unique feature allows us to work on things within our students' games all while in the playing environment.

If you are lucky enough to have a place similar to ours or if you can get on the course when no one else is around play this game called Line 'Em Up.

Game

First, pick a small target that you will hit to with every shot. If you're on the course and can see one of the stripes of grass on the fairway made by the mower, use it as your target line. Try to get each ball to land on that mow stripe or within a few mow stripes on either side.

If you're not on the course, just pick a target on the range. Hit each club in your bag once starting with your shortest iron and working all the way through your driver. The goal is to get all of your shots to end up in as straight of a line as possible. While a straight line is highly unlikely, notice how far off line your shots are from the center line or target. Use a left and right boundary on the range as your gauge for acceptability and plot your results on a piece of paper if you'd like and add that to your journal. You may start to see a pattern to the direction of your shots or that a particular club tends to be different than the others. In the latter case, you should have that club checked to make sure it was built to the same specifications as the rest of your set.

Can't Leave Until...

This can be a game that really gets under your skin. It can be frustrating to not reach your goal so make sure that is attainable. Doing so will give you some confidence. Later on, after you've reached it, you can give yourself a more challenging one.

A few examples of how to use this game could be:

- *Can't leave until you get so many into the imaginary fairway.*
- *Can't leave until you get a perfect score on the Five Ball Mental Game.*
- *Can't leave until you reach your goal on all of the shots within the Every Green game.*
- *Maybe your friend beat you at Call The Shot because you can't hook the ball. Tell yourself that you Can't leave until you've learned how to do so.*

chapter 12

ON-COURSE GAMES

The ideal hole is surely one that affords the greatest pleasure to the greatest number, gives the fullest advantage for accurate play, stimulates players to improve their game, and never becomes monotonous.

— Alister MacKenzie,
from his 1920 book *Golf Architecture*

Three Clubs & a Putter

DOEN'T USE OFTEN (handwritten)

Choosing only three clubs in addition to your putter makes you think about the holes on your home course and which clubs you can do without, which clubs you can make work and which clubs are definitely necessary.

Take for instance a par 3 hole that is 200 yards in length with the last 100 yards being water. To add to the difficulty, there is water on all sides of this green. If you decide as two of your three clubs to be a 3-wood and 7-iron, your 7-iron will likely not be able to carry a full 200 yards. So what third club will allow you, after you hit your first shot 80-90 yards, to hit a 110-120 yard second shot? This would be an important hole to plan out but you also must mix into that three club choice all of the other holes, the yardages, the layout and any possible bailout areas. After a careful recollection of the holes on your course, choose the three you feel will most benefit you.

Game

This game forces you to hit shots of varying length with the same club. In turn creating an enhanced sense of feel for the length, pace, rhythm and timing of your swing and body motion. It will become evident that bogey can be a great score. You'll learn how to and when to take a bogey and run to the next hole. Not having all of your clubs limits your shot options which should help you learn that going for broke more often than not turns a big number into an even bigger number.

This game is played in men's and ladies' clubs around the country and interestingly enough, people in these leagues do surprisingly well. Perhaps it is low expectations or that with fewer clubs the club selection process isn't so overwhelming. But playing this game will help develop your versatility which you can use next time you find yourself in an awkward situation during an actual fourteen club round of golf.

> *There are few methods of practice as valuable as making a round of the links with a single club.*
> --Harry Vardon

Flagstick Drawback

THIS ON-COURSE GAME CAN BE PLAYED with any number of people. While it will test your short game skills, it is your approach shot to the green when this Flagstick Drawback game demands a sound strategy and accurate shots.

Game

If your approach shot comes to rest within the length of the flagstick then you may proceed from there. If your approach shot ends up outside the length of the flagstick, as it did in the first photo, then you must pick up that ball and drop it ten feet off of the green, as seen in the second photo, keeping the position of where your approach shot originally resided and the flagstick in line. This may put you in the rough, in a bush, under a tree, in the fairway, on an uneven lie or in a hazard. Wherever this drop takes you is where you play the ball from.

While this game will make you choose the flag as your target, as you go along you'll learn that it's difficult to hit your approach within the length of a typical flagstick. Therefore choosing a certain side of the flag becomes important so that if need be,  you can drawback your ball to a safe side of the green away from hazards or other obstacles that will hinder your ability to get up-and-down.

You can play this game keeping score by the traditional method of counting each stroke you take or by the following process. You get five points if your approach comes to rest with the length of the flagstick. You can give yourself two points for an approach that resides on the green yet outside the length of the flagstick and one point if you successfully get up-and-down regardless of what it's for. By giving yourself a point for getting up-and-down regardless of whether it's for par, bogey, or double you will be training your mindset to get up-and-down no matter what score it is for. It's about taking pride in yourself and your own game. If you walk off the golf course that day having shot the worst score you've posted in a long time but you took pride and went through your routine, stayed focused and encouraged then you are destined for greatness. That is a challenge to live by but with this approach to the game you'll likely save many strokes and if you play in multiple day tournaments or on a golf team you know how important this is. You can bet that that terrible score you just posted would have been more embarrassing had you taken on a negative attitude.

Two Ball Game

YOU WILL NOT GET BETTER by taking mulligans. They go directly against what the essence of the game really should be teaching us. That mulligan or second try that you take typically isn't a better swing it's a swing made without the pressures of the first ball. And you can't do it on your first ball because you always have had that second ball ready to go. It's a redo that gives you a false sense of accomplishment. Champions don't want "do overs." They want to prove to themselves that they can do it on the first ball and if their first shot is less than desirable they'll show themselves on their approach, they'll show themselves how to recover if need be, they'll show themselves they can make par from anywhere. They take pride in chasing around that first ball and getting it into the hole. Mulligans aren't part of their game or vocabulary.

Game

This Two Ball Game is just the opposite of getting a mulligan. While you get to hit two balls, you must always choose the less desirable shot until both balls are holed. From the tee on a par 4, let's say one ball is driven right down the middle and the other is in the fairway bunker. Pick up the ball in the fairway and place it in the bunker with the other ball. Proceed by hitting both balls from there. If one ends up on the green and the other ends up twenty yards short, then again hit two balls from that twenty yard pitch. Continue until there isn't a worse shot meaning both balls end up in the hole. This can take additional time, so it's wise to play by yourself or in a twosome. It is also recommended that you have extra golf balls available so that you can drop one next to the worst ball and pick up your better ball as you progress toward the green.

In the photo I drove one ball into the fairway and another in the left rough putting me behind these trees. I proceeded by hitting two shots from this location having to hook them around the trees and toward the green. I continued this process of hitting two balls and picking the worst one throughout the entire hole.

Psych 101

One of the easiest ways to improve your play and score is by bettering your on-course game. To improve your on-course game, look to your routine. More specifically, look to the part of your routine that should be evaluating the shot in front of you. Look to the mental part that helps you commit and execute the shot.

Similar to the Five Ball Mental Game found in the Full Swing chapter, this game is devised strictly for the golf course. Challenge yourself mentally and see your scores and enjoyment of the game improve dramatically.

Game

This game that you play on the golf course has three possible points for each shot you hit. The first point relates to your complete evaluation of the shot at hand. Evaluate all of the items that are required to choose an appropriate target, club and shot. If your evaluation was thorough then give yourself a point.

Then after pulling that club, you need to commit fully to it, your target and the type of shot. You may find that you have a mental trigger that tells yourself you're focused, committed and ready to swing. It should be something that helps you only care about what you're doing at that time. A student shared with me that over a full swing shot after he looks at the target a few times his eyes go one last time slowly and deliberately from the ball to the target. In doing so he realizes that he doesn't see anything else or get distracted. His shot has been 100% committed to. That slow, deliberate look at the target is his mental trigger.

While your evaluation and commitment to the shot make up the first two points, the final third point is awarded based on your post-shot routine. A post-shot routine relates to a few items and here are some examples that many sports psychologists try to get their clients to adhere to.

After a shot that you don't care for, take a practice swing and visualize how you had originally imagined the shot turning out. End on that good note, put the club in the bag and proceed by readying yourself for your next shot. After a good shot, file it away into your memory by reacting to it positively. You can give yourself some small words of encouragement or a positive physical act. In future rounds and shots, this will help you recall your good shots while any remembrance of the others won't exist. I believe that everyone must find their own way that helps them perform at their best. You need to do whatever it is that helps spark your focus for your next shot. If you go through your post-shot routine in a personally beneficial manner, you can award yourself one point. You may also find during your post-shot routine that you failed to notice a factor during your evaluation of the shot. In this case, you can give yourself a point for your post-shot routine but not one for your evaluation. Use the scorecard below to grade each shot on the course.

SCORECARD

Hole / Shot	1	2	3	4	5	6	7	8	9	10	11	12	13	14	15	16	17	18
#1																		
#2																		
#3																		
#4																		
#5																		
#6																		
#7																		
Your Pt. Ttl. / Out of																		

Vary the Tee

THE SPECIFIC NAME FOR THIS GAME at our golf course is Red, Blue, Gold. These are the colors of the tees that represent the forward tees, the middle tees and the tips respectively. You can call it what you want based on your home course. The point is to play different tees that may take you out of your comfort level and to appreciate the different parts of the game that you'll need as a result of playing from tees that you're not accustomed to. For instance, a better player playing from the forward tees may need to strategize differently off of the tee hitting an iron off several of the tee boxes if a longer club would not fit the dogleg. A short hitter who plays from the tips will likely depend quite highly on a skilled short game. It doesn't necessarily matter if you shoot a great score - certainly strive for that - but the point is to stimulate different thinking. It is to develop other aspects of your game that are demanded of you due to playing the same course from a completely different set of tees. You may see and read your home course in a new way that will help you read and strategize holes and shots at other golf courses.

Game

As stated above, you will complete 18-holes from the forward tees. On a different day play the middle tees and on a separate day tee it up from the tips. This will enhance your strategy for each shot and hole. It will become evident that on a long, unreachable par 4 that you need to plan your second shot so that your third comes in from a beneficial angle and from a distance that is preferable to you. Playing from the tips may require that you do this on almost every par 4. It can be mentally draining as you attempt to get up-and-down all day but you'll persevere by knowing that this game is all about taking pride in circumstances that will wear out most of the competition - don't let yourself be one of those who breaks down.

On a flight home from Florida after being there for a college golf tournament, I caught a show on the in-flight television. Jack Nicklaus was talking about, among other things, the few days leading up to a tournament. He would read in the papers or hear about certain players complaining about the condition of the course, the long length of the course or other factors and he would simply chalk those players off his list. He knew those complainers didn't have a chance. They took themselves right out of the tournament.

If you're a longer hitter playing the forward tees, it is likely that your short game will also need to be on. If you play a narrow, tree-lined course, precision with the driver or a different strategy all together will be necessary for the longer hitter. This game is a great way to turn ON other parts of your game that may be in hibernation without you even realizing it. A variation to this game is to change the tee box for every hole you play. In other words, play the forward tees on hole #1, the next set of tees back for hole #2 and so on throughout the round. Another day, start from the tips and move forward with each hole. This will make each hole play quite differently than you're used to and hence allow you to play shots you're not accustomed to.

Odd or Even

ODD OR EVEN ENTAILS playing a round of golf with only your odd numbered clubs or only your even numbered clubs.

If you happen to carry driver, 3-wood, and 5-wood within your normal full set, then when playing with your odd clubs take out your driver and 5-wood. When playing with your even clubs, take out your 3-wood and play with the driver and 5-wood.

There are many factors that make up great players but one is their ability to hit partial shots and cover those yardages that are between clubs. Being able to take some off a shot or being able to go at one a little more are capabilities that great players have. You may find out that you're much better at swinging easier with a longer club than trying to swing harder with the shorter club. Some find it to be just the opposite. That going at one harder is much more productive than trying to smooth one up there. Such information will be found out with some experimentation.

Odd or Even demands this of you as you stand in the fairway evaluating the shot knowing that a 7-iron is the club but only having a 6-iron and an 8-iron. It will enhance your ability to read the shot. Ask yourself, *Would I rather be short or would I rather be long?* You have to evaluate an appropriate place for each shot to end up.

It may be that you need to hit the longer club purposely landing the ball a bit past the hole risking going over but knowing that a shot that comes to rest over the green makes for an easier up-and-down than one that comes up short. Things like the shape of the green, hole location or hazards all need to be considered. This effective type of thinking will trickle down into your regular play when you have all of your clubs.

Play this game of Odd or Even a few times over the course of the season using whichever clubs you didn't the time before. You can also use this game with a slight variation changing between odd and even clubs during the round. For instance, during the same round play with even numbered clubs on the even numbered holes and your odd clubs on the odd numbered holes.

Two Ball Score

The game of golf requires concentration and attention. Luckily you don't have to do this all of the time. There is a lot of time between shots when you don't have to be as focused. Some people however play their best when they put the blinders on and are more into their round throughout the entire time that it takes to complete 18-holes. Others play their best when, between shots, they let their mind wander. Whichever method works best for you, you do need to focus on the task at hand at the right time. If you lack concentration then this game will challenge you at first. But with a realization as to your need to properly focus on the process of each shot perhaps you'll develop a trigger that kick starts your attention to the details that each shot requires. This mental transition is crucial and with it comes more consistent results and more successful rounds. It's a healthy approach to playing.

Game

You may need to play by yourself or with only one other person for pace of play reasons. Play an entire round of golf hitting two balls. Wherever they go is where you play each one from. Continue until both balls are holed. Add the two scores together on each hole to come up with a two ball score for the hole. You may make a four with one ball and a six with the other. In this case your score would be a ten on that hole. Continue this two ball game for the remainder of the round.

Playing a round of Two Ball Score is more challenging than playing with one ball. You're likely to end up mentally exhausted but know that you'll be a stronger player in the future for doing it. Over time it will enhance your level of concentration and make a normal round with one ball seem easier and that's why you practice.

EMPHASIS

THIS IS A PERFECT GAME when you're preparing yourself for a tournament. Perhaps you know what the tournament course looks like but you can't get there to play or practice it until closer to the tournament day. Instead you play your home course and set some rules to make it seem more similar to the course you'll be playing in the tournament.

Emphasis is a game in which you put a premium on a certain aspect of the game. If the golf course that you're preparing for has tall rough around the greens or a great number of bunkers guarding the greens, you would want to put an emphasis on hitting greens in regulation.

In another example, in preparing a Division I golf team for a competitive away tournament in which the course was tight off the tee, the head coach and I decided to put an emphasis on hitting fairways. Even though this was a round played at the team's home course which isn't narrow, it prepared the team for what they would encounter come tournament time.

GAME

In the college example above, Emphasis was played by adding one half of a stroke for any tee shot that didn't hit the fairway. While the player may get his or her ball out of the rough and save a par, on the actual golf course where the tournament will be held, the lack of hitting the fairway would likely lead to a bogey. Even though you may have an accomplished short game and the versatility of hitting recovery shots, it's difficult to scramble all day from the woods.

As stated above, Emphasis can be played in several ways. Another is to add one half stroke for any shot that misses the green and another half stroke for a missed fairway. At St. Andrews in Scotland where the bunkers are treacherous, an additional half stroke is generous.

Ideally, you'll get the opportunity to practice and play at the tournament course before hand but if not, make up a game of Emphasis at your home course that resembles what you'll be encountering. If you don't know any of the characteristics to the course you'll be playing, call ahead. There's always some pro or member willing to share some local knowledge.

1 point fairway
2 pts greens
1 pt up/down
+.5 1 putt
+1 pt acceptance

-½ miss fairway
-1 pt haxard/dothead
-2 pt adonce only
-3 penalty
-4 stroke/distance
-2 pts negative thoughts

total points

No Driver *on Primary*

TEACHING AT A GOLF COURSE I'm lucky to be able to witness the behavior of people playing and the tee shot is obviously one of the most unplanned shots in golf. People who have never played the golf course will drive their cart to the tee box and immediately pull the driver out of the bag without a care for what the hole looks like, how it was designed and what type of shot the architecture dictates. This behavior is such a habit to some that I've witnessed on several occasions players stepping up to a short par 3 hole with driver in their hands because it's what they always take to the tee. They fail to look at the hole and the shot, matching it to their ability before they pull a club. It's the wrong approach to playing if improving your score is of any interest to you.

It is quite common to hear tour players these days talk about hitting it as far as possible and wherever it goes is secondary. This is more valid for them because they have unbelievable skills when it comes to recovering from the spots they put themselves in. Many junior golfers also tend to swing for the fences and learn to control it later. The problem with taking this approach and applying it to the general public is that the weekend duffer doesn't have as technically sound of a swing as tour pros. Every shot in golf demands a plan that will enable your miss-hits to be acceptable and not penal. Have a plan that makes sense. This game will hopefully open your mind as to the strategy of each shot and how the architect designed the hole to be played consequently bettering your thinking, your risk-reward analysis and your game management.

GAME

No Driver means to take it completely out of your bag and play a round of golf whether it be nine or eighteen. You can even put a twist to the game by not allowing the use of any woods. An all iron round of golf, as seen in the photo. It will make you look at the hole more strategically, more precisely and you'll likely score better. You'll probably hit more fairways and lose less golf balls. If you struggle at courses other than your home course, it may be because you've become so accustomed to playing your own course that strategizing ceases to exist. You know the course too well. One great way to break out of that redundancy is to play the course without a driver or without your woods. You'll find yourself in completely different places on the course and consequently you'll have to strategize and think your way around.

Using your other clubs off the tee will make you develop a plan. You may have to hit a long iron off of the tee and a long iron to the green on a particular par 4 hole. Yet on another hole you may find that you can still have a short iron into the green as you did with your driver but that your long iron is more accurate and puts you at a better angle in which to come into the green. In short, taking away the driver or all of the woods, depending on which version you wish to play, will open up the course to a whole new light.

> *There should be infinite variety in the strokes required to play the various holes.*
>
> -- Alister MacKenzie,
> from his 1920 book *Golf Architecture*

Good Practice Round Game

Pins

9 Hole
Pins 18 Hole

If you can honestly evaluate your game you will be more likely to pinpoint what needs attention and more likely to then improve those areas. In order to get a clearer picture of this, I have many of my students chart each shot they hit during a round. Much valuable information can be found from this process. Let's take for instance, a player who finds out he commonly comes up short of the green on his approach shots. This can be, among other things, due to a lack of properly evaluating all of the factors that go into a shot or perhaps the player has a dishonest view of how far he hits each of his clubs.

Whatever the reason is for your chronic miss, Pins will encourage you to think and play the game differently. It will put a stop to the constant ailment that is afflicting your game.

Game

If a particular golfer is chronically hitting his approach shots short of the green or simply too far short of the pin, then Pins is used to give the player a point for every approach shot that ends up past the pin even if it travels over the green. This is of course unless a hazard or other trouble lurks over the green. Then the hole is played without the point system. If on an 18-hole course, there are three holes in which trouble awaits just over the green then the maximum point total would be fifteen. No points are given out on those three holes as it makes no sense for a person to fire toward the back part of the green if a penalty is likely. Feel free to keep your stroke total as you regularly would but really put emphasis on the points you receive for going past the pin on the appropriate holes. The objective of this game is to get over the fear of going long, of hitting it too far or of being too aggressive.

You can use Pins for various reasons. Many older, traditional courses have circular greens that slope severely from back to front. Going long on such greens makes for a challenging up-and-down so you can alter the game and give yourself a point for being short of the pin. You can even add tighter standards like you must be short of the pin but on the green. If you have knowledge of the pin locations for that day and are familiar with the course, you can designate hole by hole what side of the pin you should hit toward and award yourself a point for doing so.

+1   +1   FAT SIDE OF PIN

Pins can also be used to hit to the left or right side of the pin. If on hole one, the pin is tucked to the right side of the green, as seen in the photo, a point can be awarded for hitting your approach to the left side of it. If on hole two, the pin is tucked up front with a hazard in front, this demands a shot that goes past the pin and a point should be awarded for accomplishing this. Keep in mind that playing to the apparent safe side of a pin indeed may not be safe after a better view of the green's surroundings. You'll have to plan accordingly. Sometimes going directly at the pin is the right plan.

This game can also be used for pitching the ball, chipping the ball and even putting. Overall, it will help you see the most advantageous position for where the next shot should be played.

Points

THIS GAME IS A COMPLETELY DIFFERENT way of calculating points while playing a round of golf. Compared to the traditional method of counting strokes, this game of Points will reward steady play and low scores while decreasing your point total for those dreadful big numbers.

While it's important to be ready for any circumstance that may come your way during a round of golf, steady golf is easy golf. Steady golf is often boring to better players. But the steadiness to hitting fairway after fairway and green after green is awarded in this game and it will take righting the ship if you falter a bit.

Game

You will be awarding yourself points for almost every shot you hit. Feel free to alter the point value of certain topics if you feel one of them is more valuable based on the course you play. If birdies are hard to come by at your course, you can up their value. If you want to make a three-putt more of a penalty, change its value to a minus three. If bogey is a good score for you, change its worth.

Topic	Points
Fairway Hit (from tee)	1
Fairway Hit (on 2nd shot Par 5)	1 [2]
Green Hit	1 [2]
Par	1 [2]
Birdie	2 [3]
Eagle	4
Chip in	2 [1]
Bogey	-2
Double Bogey	-4
Triple Bogey or Worse	-5
Up-and-Down (regardless of what it's for)	+2
Three putt	-2 [-3]

Reverse Scramble

In this game called reverse scramble, groups of equal number play against each other. This most commonly takes place in teams of two so that two teams can play together rounding out a foursome.

In the typical scramble format each person hits their first shot. The team chooses the best shot out of the group and then they all hit from that spot. They continue this process all the way through the hole choosing the best shot each time until one is holed.

You've probably guessed what Reverse Scramble is by now. It is the opposite approach. Instead of choosing the best shot, the group must choose the worst shot. Regardless of group size, each member of the team hits their first shot. From the group's first shots, the worst one must be chosen. All members of the team proceed from that spot. After hitting from there, the team must again choose the worst shot and hit from there. This is done throughout the hole until one member of the team knocks one into the hole. Once someone puts one in the hole the hole is over for that team. The team with the lowest stroke total is the winner.

This game puts a lot of pressure on every member of the team. You must count penalty strokes as well. If in a two player team, Player A smokes one down the middle of the fairway on a par 4 and his teammate proceeds to knock one out of bounds, they both must tee off again. In this case and based on the rules of golf they're hitting three from the tee box. This isn't a game I would promote to higher handicap golfers. It can take a while to play. It is great for low handicap golfers as they hit very few stray shots. The pressures of this game often multiply so if a big tournament is on the horizon, this can be a good pressure-packed game to use as preparation.

About the Author

Trent Wearner, the 2004 Colorado PGA Teacher of the Year, is recognized nationally by *Golf Magazine* as one of the Top Teachers in the Southwestern United States as well as by *Golf Digest* as one of the Best Teachers in the State and has most recently been nominated for *Golf Magazine's* Top 100 Teachers in the country for 2007-2008.

He teaches and coaches players of all ability levels including many of the top middle school, high school and college players in the region. You can find him at the Meridian Golf Learning Center in Englewood, Colorado.

To learn more about golf schools, private lessons, corporate golf opportunities or speaking engagements please visit www.TrentWearnerGolf.com

TRENT WEARNER
PGA PROFESSIONAL